ADVANCE COMMENTS FOR ...

Having served in the military for over 27 years, I've always been interested in the history of World War II. Gary Slaughter has pulled together stories only available as a small part of WWII history. He covers POWs capture, escape attempts-successes and failures, treatment by guards, health, activities, statistics and much more. I was interested to learn about German, Italian and Japanese treatment of Allied POWs as compared to those Axis POWs imprisoned in the United States. I was not aware, but not surprised, at how well these prisoners were treated. Many were befriended by those American civilians living near the encampments. The book was concise and quickly read with facts easily consumed and understood. Whether you are a war historian or just someone wanting to know more about how POWs survived or died, this book is for you.

CAPT James V. Hunt, USN (Ret.), Mayor City of Belle Meade, TN

Slaughter takes us to a world-wide view of the millions of WWII POWs. He details the astounding difference between Allied-run camps and those of the Axis powers. This informative document sheds light on an area of history bypassed by the conventional WW II histories.

LT Karl (Chuck) Nuechterlein, USNR (Ret.)

Gary Slaughter's *WWII POWS in America and Abroad* is quite a departure from his previous works, offering a look at prisoners of war during the second world war ... not only in the US, but in other countries. His five *Cottonwood* novels were set in a slightly fictionalized Owosso, Michigan, (his hometown) during WWII and followed the war and the capers of Jase and Danny, two local boys. His autobiographical work, *Sea Stories,* reflected upon his time as a Naval officer from 1956-67. *Journey of an Inquiring Mind* traced his transformation to a novelist.

Josh Champlin, *Argus-Press* Staff Writer, Owosso, MI

WW II POWs is constructed with bites of information, along with anecdotes. The book is an easy read that can be picked up and put down without fear of losing the thread of the work. Anecdote leave you with a warm feeling about Americans and their conduct, even in those difficult of times when virtually every one had someone fighting in the war.

CDR Andrew A. Bradick, USN (Ret.)

A fascinating collection of facts and narratives related to World War II incarcerations. Slaughter has researched both civilian and military camps, chronicling experiences on both the Allies' and the Axis Powers' sides. There is definite relevance, even so many years later. This is not necessarily a book to read straight through, but rather one to leaf through time and again for new perspectives on war captivity.

Ruth Beaumont Cook, Author of *Guests Behind the Barbed Wire.*

Gary Slaughter has presented a very interesting account of little-known events in the history of the Second World War. During this war, I lived in San Francisco, but I was never aware of anyone from the city leaving for internment camps. When I learned of the imprisonment of US citizens of Japanese ancestry in internment camps, I was shocked and angry. I most highly recommend *WW II POWs ...* a most informative work.

CAPT Paul Goorjian, USN (Ret.)

Though I was born in Owosso, Michigan after WWII, I never knew about Camp Owosso until decades later. It is very difficult to understand why so little was written about this captivating topic. Slaughter brings this subject to life like a spy novel, as he weaves the stories with information and data so adeptly that it is difficult to put the book down.

Piper E. Brewer, Director Shiawassee Arts Center, Owosso, MI

Gary Slaughter's history of the people interned during WWII shines a light on the little-known events that brought tens of thousands of enemy soldiers into America's heartland, after the US entered the war. Interesting are the government's efforts that led to POWs volunteering, for pay, to work on farms and in factories, thereby helping the US war efforts. Then, after the war, returning the POWs, healthy and better educated, to assist war torn Europe's democratic restoration. Also documented is the government's unjust internment of innocent US citizens. *WWII POWs in America and Abroad* is a needed examination of how and why America responded to the enemy, real and perceived, in the homeland during WWII.

LT Les Westerman, USNR (Ret.)

ACCLAIM FOR ...

"*Sea Stories: A Memoir of a Naval Officer 1956-1967* contains vignettes recounting episodes from Gary Slaughter's life serving on destroyers during the Cold War. All these encounters are given equal billing to an extraordinary event during the Cuban missile crisis when our hero had to face up to an emotional captain of a Soviet submarine armed with nuclear weapons. This is heady stuff and one of those lost stories of the Cold War well worth knowing. These vignettes add up to a very real story that is neither gung-ho or shallow. The book has comedy, tragedy, and drama in equal measure."
War History Online, Mark Barnes, August 2016

"Shedding light on some of the most infamous conflicts in United States history during the Cold War, Gary Slaughter shares his recollections of his direct involvement in *Sea Stories: A Memoir of a Naval Officer (1956-1967)*, a gripping collection of vignettes fusing the optimism, morality, and patriotism of the era with hard facts and grim realities of naval warfare. Taken as a collection of short stories or altogether, Sea *Stories,* is sure to capture attention of historians everywhere."
Foreword Reviews, Pallas Gates McCorquodale, August 2016

"There are many classic books about combat in WW II (*The Naked and the Dead, From Here to Eternity*, etc.) and perhaps far fewer about life back home in the United States. But the home front is a specialty of the author who grew up in a small-town during Wartime. *Cottonwood Summer '45* by Gary Slaughter is an engrossing story, and even though today's times are far different from the 1940s, readers will also go away wondering if they could and would act in similar fashion under the same circumstances. Slaughter makes a convincing case that heroes are not always found fighting a shooting War."
US Review of Books, Eric Hoffer Awards, May 2012

"*Cottonwood Spring* is a fun, easy read, laced with fact and fiction. Among real characters that turn up along the way are New York Governor Thomas E. Dewey, Foreign Service Officer Alvin M. Bentley, and Owosso Mayor J. Edwin Ellis. In the meantime, Jase and Danny manage to get into and out of trouble in the fictional town of Riverton, a thinly disguised Owosso."
Owosso Argus-Press, March 2009

"*Cottonwood Winter: A Christmas Story* is an upbeat portrayal of a simpler nation united around common goals."
Nashville Scene (Our Critics Pick), November 2007

"*Cottonwood Fall* is an especially engaging novel recalling a vivid depiction of America during the difficult year of 1944. Slaughter's unique writing style is sure to consume the readers' attention as *Cottonwood Fall* follows two ten-year old boys through their adventures in a small town, Riverton, Michigan. *Cottonwood Fall* is highly recommended to the general reader, especially those intrigued by the World War II lifestyle of the American citizen."
Midwest Book Review, March 2006

"*Cottonwood Summer* documents author Gary Slaughter, an undeniably talented writer, as a master at creating loveable characters and an engaging story-telling narrative enriched with humor and originality. *Cottonwood Summer* is a mystery with Nazi spies, nasty POWs, undercover moles, small-town values, and Gold Star mothers who will never see their sons again. Irreverent, touching, and a reader-involving story, *Cottonwood Summer* is one of those novels so easy to pick up and so hard to put down."
Midwest Book Review, May 2004

Also, by Gary Slaughter

Fiction

Cottonwood Summer '45

Cottonwood Spring

Cottonwood Winter: A Christmas Story

Cottonwood Fall

Cottonwood Summer

Non-Fiction

Sea Stories: A Memoir of a Naval Officer (1956-1967)

The Journey of an Inquiring Mind:
From Scholar, Naval Officer, and Entrepreneur to Novelist
with Joanne Fletcher Slaughter

WW II POWs
in America and Abroad

Layout and design: Publish & Launch
Cover design: Damonza.com
Publicity: Books Forward

Publisher's Cataloging-in-Publication Data
Names: Slaughter, Gary, author. | Slaughter, Joanne Fletcher, editor.
Title: WW II POWs in America and abroad/ by Gary Slaughter; edited by
    Joanne Fletcher Slaughter.
Description: Nashville, TN: Fletcher House, 2021. | Illustrated; 40 b&w photos. |
    Summary: The United States imprisoned its own citizens in camps throughout
    America—over 100,000 Japanese-Americans and 11,500 German-Americans—
    most naturalized U.S. citizens. Like military camps, these civilian sites were also
    surrounded by barbed wire and guard towers.
Identifiers: LCCN 2020918340 | ISBN 9781733802130 (pbk.) | ISBN
    9781733802147 (epub) | ISBN 9781733802154 (mobi)
Subjects: LCSH: Concentration camp inmates. | Detention of persons. | World War,
    1939-1945 – Concentration camps. | World War, 1939-1945 -- Evacuation of
    civilians. | World War, 1939-1945 – Prisoners and prisons. | BISAC: HISTORY /
    Military / World War II. | HISTORY / United States / 20th Century. | HISTORY /
    Europe / General.
Classification: LCC D805.A2 S53 2020 (print) | LCC D805.A2 (ebook)
    | DDC 940.54--dc23
LC record available at https://lccn.loc.gov/2020918340

Published by Fletcher House
Nashville, TN

Our gratitude to those who have followed the POW storylines in the Cottonwood *Series and who have expressed interest in knowing more about POWs — military and civilian — during World War II. Your many questions during book talks stimulated us to research and compile this book.*

Our prayers that our grandchildren and your grandchildren and generations to follow will never live through this era that we and your grandparents did.

A typical prisoner of war internment camp in the United States during World War II. *Photo from the National Archives. Identifier: 539960.*

CONTENTS

The National Prisoner of War Museum in Andersonville, Georgia. Former prisoners of war partnered with Andersonville National Historic Site to create and develop the National Prisoner of War Museum, the only museum solely dedicated to interpreting the American prisoner of war experience. Opening in 1998, the National Prisoner of War Museum is dedicated to all prisoners of war in America's past who have served their country with dignity and distinction, so that current and future generations will be inspired by their service and sacrifice. *Photo from* <u>*www.nps.gov*</u>

WW II POWs
in America and Abroad

by
Gary Slaughter

with

Joanne Fletcher Slaughter

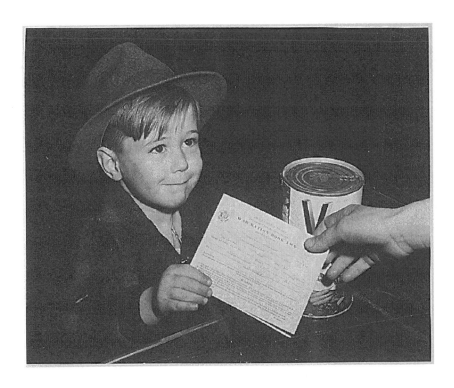

An eager school boy gets his first experience in using War Ration Book Two. With many parents engaged in war work, children are being taught the facts of point rationing for helping out in family shopping. *Photo from the National Archives. Identifier: 53556*

Introduction

When I was growing up in Owosso, Michigan, I observed captured German POWs *up-close-and-personally.* Yes, in the early 1940s, I saw POWs, interned at Camp Owosso, right in my own neighborhood. This chance encounter would later fuel my passionate interest in the subject of POWs during WW II in America and abroad.

Compared with most other events that occurred during the War, relatively little is written about this sizeable chapter in the War's history. And in the early 2000s, I decided to write about this period.

In 2004, my first novel, *Cottonwood Summer*, was published. Four more novels followed, each one set in the last four seasons of the War and detailing life on the home front, as seen through the eyes of two nine-year old boys. (See Appendix C: *Historical Events of World War II).*

Drawing on my early memory of POWs, each book contains POW storylines. To read a few POW storylines from each of the five novels, see Chapter 13. *POW-Related Excerpts from the* Cottonwood *novels.*

The stories are narrated by Jase Addison, based on myself in Riverton, Michigan, a fictionalized version of Owosso. My best friend and constant companion, Billy Curtis, is Danny Tucker, the main character of the five books. The German POWs in these books are based on factual information gleaned from my study of the subject and from my actual observations and experiences with German POWs who were imprisoned in nearby Camp Owosso.

After the publication of *Cottonwood Summer,* readers and attendees at my *Behind the Book* talks expressed interest in learning more about POWs. To answer these questions credibly, I diligently researched and studied this subject.

In 2006, I introduced a twenty-five-minute talk, entitled *POWs in America: 1943-1946.* Since then, I have presented this talk to hundreds of highly interested audiences all over the country.

Through the years, I have assembled a sizable library of newspaper articles, white papers, and books written about POWs in America during the War. Also, I was fortunate that my business took me to Germany, where I encountered former German soldiers who, during their younger years, spent time in American POW camps. Their eagerness to share stories further encouraged me to research, speak, and write on this subject.

Why the appeal? There are two major reasons.

First, there were some 940 permanent POW camps in America during the War between 1943 and 1946. These camps were dispersed widely throughout forty-six of the forty-eight states back then. Some of those in my audiences were old enough to have observed POWs as I did. Like me, they too were eager to share their POW experiences and observations with others.

Second, those who were not old enough to have personally observed POWs were generally incredulous when first hearing about the 435,000 German, Italian, and Japanese POWs interned here in America. They wanted to know more.

But, why is this subject so unfamiliar to most Americans? When the POWs were repatriated after the War, all records of their internment in America were sent back with them to their countries of origin. However, POWs leaving America did not return to their homes immediately. They were delayed by our European allies to rebuild those countries that had been damaged badly by enemy forces. So, the first German, Italian, and Japanese POWs arrived in America in 1943 and did not return to their home countries until some years after their departure from America in 1946.

Hundreds of history books have been written about World War II, but historians have had great difficulty finding information about POWs. In fact, during the period between 2002 and 2006, I only found five other books on the subject of POWs in America during the War:

- Cook, Ruth Beaumont, *Guests Behind the Barbed Wire*, Crane Hill Publishers, 2006.
- Cowley, Betty, *Stalag Wisconsin*, Badger Books, Inc., 2002.
- Gansberg, Judith M., *Stalag USA.*, Thomas Y. Crowell Company, 1977.
- Kramer, Arnold, *Nazi Prisoners of War in America*, Scarborough House/Publishers, 1996.
- Robin, Ron, *The Barbed-Wire College*, Princeton University Press, 1995.

I felt fortunate to be included among those few authors who researched and wrote about this relatively unknown chapter in the history of World War II.

The books that I mentioned above differ greatly from my current work, because they are basically anecdotal accounts that describe situations and activities involving individual POWs.

Instead, I have recounted the history of this phenomenon and focused on the big picture, as well as on the American government's policies and procedures in the imprisonment of German, Italian, and Japanese POWs in over 900 camps in America.

As I researched, I quickly became aware that, in addition to the WWII camps in America, both the Allied Forces and the Axis Powers had confined their own civilians, in addition to the captured military prisoners. These camps included internment and concentration camps, as well as death camps.

Immediately following the War, the Nuremberg Trials for Axis leaders provided a small measure of retributive justice for their atrocities committed against humanity.

I am very grateful for the excellent reporting of our Allied War correspondents and for the extremely comprehensive photographical history of the War compiled by the National Archives. For a visual frame of reference, please refer to *Appendix D: Photographic Scenes from World War II*.

"Children of an eastern suburb of London, who have been made homeless by the random bombs of the Nazi night raiders, waiting outside the wreckage of what was their home." September 1940. 306-NT-3163V. *Photo from the National Archives. Identifier: 541920.*

"A prisoner of war is a man who tries to kill you and fails, and then asks you not to kill him."

Sir Winston Churchill

1. The German-American Experience

During World War II, German POWs in America and ordinary American citizens enjoyed amiable relations to a great extent.

Several reasons account for this extraordinary good relationship between Americans and the POWs whom they came to know as POWs worked in forests, on their farms, or side by side with them in our factories.

These POWs were different from some of their peers in the German army. They were much younger than expected. Most prisoners working for Americans during the War were in their late teens or early twenties. They were extremely relieved to be in America even under these conditions rather than the unpleasant alternatives, including dreadful conditions their counterparts were experiencing fighting the Soviets in the dead of winter in snow and ice-covered fields of Russia. On the contrary, they lived relatively comfortably and were content as POWs in America during the War.

These men ate well. Their quarters were more than adequate. Their guards, for the most part, were kind and considerate, but above all else, POWs were paid well for the hours they worked. All these factors led to uniformly pleasant dispositions of these young German POWs.

The average young German POW had a very good physique, a handsome head of blond hair, and vivid blue eyes. They were known for having a fine mind, positive disposition, and friendly manner.

Aside from the fact that they were the *enemy*, what was not to like?

They loved being here, and Americans loved having them here as well. The country needed their help, and they were eager to supply it – and they were liked and admired.

However, a small percentage of POWs in America were older, dedicated Nazis, angered by having been captured by the Allies. Fortunately, they were isolated in separate, more secure, and harsher POW camps away from the younger men.

The Nazification of German Americans

During the 1930s, a number of pro-German groups existed in America. These nationalistic organizations usually were organized and led by Germans who immigrated to America after the first world war. Nominally they claimed as their purpose such lofty ideals as the encouragement of friendship and trade between Germany and America or the preservation of Germanic culture in America through the study and exhibition of history, art, music, and literature.

Like the National Socialist (Nazi) party in Germany, these German-American organizations sought to gain political power. They created semi-military branches to intimidate and strong-arm their political foes. Many groups were fervently pro-Nazi and anti-Semitic in their beliefs and practices. As such, they became fronts for espionage and subversive activities against America before and during World War II.

At the insistence of Hitler himself, these disparate organizations were consolidated as the *American-German Bund*. Their Hitler-appointed leader and self-proclaimed American Fuhrer was Fritz Julius Kuhn. During World War I, like Hitler himself, Kuhn earned the Iron Cross while serving as an infantry lieutenant. This medal is the German equivalent to our Congressional Medal of Honor. Unlike Hitler, after the first War, Kuhn graduated from the University of Munich with a Master's Degree in Chemical Engineering and then moved to America, where he became a naturalized citizen in 1934.

In 1939, at the height of its popularity, the Bund held a rally in Madison Square Garden attended by some 20,000 people. They listened to speeches by Kuhn in which he referred to FDR as *Frank D. Rosenfeld* and called Roosevelt's New Deal, the *Jew Deal*. Predictably violence broke out between Jewish protestors and Bund storm troopers, who wore uniforms to emulate their German counterparts, the Sturmabteilung (SA), also known as *Brown Shirts* because of the color of their uniforms.

Seeking to topple the leadership of the Bund, New York City Mayor Fiorello La Guardia launched an investigation of the Bund's taxes. It revealed that Kuhn had embezzled thousands of dollars from the organization, much of which was spent on his mistress.

District Attorney Thomas E. Dewey indicted Kuhn and won a conviction against him. Later Dewey went on to be governor of New York and was twice nominated as the Republican candidate for President of the United States.

Author's Note. Governor Dewey was born and raised in Owosso, Michigan. He attended Owosso High School and the University of Michigan.

When World War II broke out, Kuhn was arrested as an enemy agent and held as a prisoner until the War ended. Subsequently he was transported to Ellis Island and deported to Germany. Most Bund members were similarly interned and deported after the War.

During World War II, about 125,000 Japanese Americans were interned in relocation camps in the western states. And nearly 11,000 German Americans were also interned as enemy aliens and some of them were not released until as late as 1948, at least two years later than their Japanese counterparts. Serious abuses of civil liberties were proven in cases involving both groups of internees.

Clash between Hardened Nazis and Non-Nazi POWs

The hard-won successes of the Allies in North Africa, Sicily, and Italy brought with them a number of challenging problems. Among the most difficult was how to manage the hundreds of thousands of captured German and Italian soldiers, airmen, and sailors who were entitled to the privileges and benefits accorded to Prisoners of War by the Geneva Convention.

The Geneva Conventions comprise four treaties and three more protocols that establish the standards of international law for humanitarian treatment during war. The singular term *Geneva Convention* usually denotes the agreements of 1949, negotiated in the aftermath of World War II (1939–1945), which updated the terms of the two 1929 treaties and added two new conventions.

The Geneva Conventions extensively

- defined the basic rights of wartime prisoners (civilians and military personnel),
- established protections for the wounded and sick, and
- established protections for the civilians in and around a war-zone.

The treaties of 1949 were ratified by 196 countries. The Geneva Convention also defines the rights and protections of non-combatants. The Geneva Convention does not address the use of weapons, which is the subject of the Hague Conventions.

Dealing with the sheer numbers of POWs was an enormous headache. In America, we provided facilities and personnel to accommodate over 379,000 German POWs alone. This doesn't include thousands of Italians, Japanese, and other members of the Axis forces who were also turned over to us.

The German prisoners were particularly difficult to manage. Since the early 1930s, when Hitler and his National Socialists came to power, young Germans had been brainwashed by a pervasive, insidious, but extremely effective propaganda machine. The mass brainwashing of the German citizenry is acknowledged as the most successful in history. (This of course depends on how one defines *success*.) Even highly educated, open-minded German citizens were systematically converted into arrogant, racist, and belligerent Nazi zealots because of the sinister bombardment of propaganda.

Nazism's hold over German soldiers did not end when they became prisoners of war. Captured Nazi leaders forced their fellow POWs to resist all attempts by their American captors to lessen the power and influence of Nazism in our prison camps. At first, Nazism thrived among the POWs, making it difficult for the U.S. Army Military Police to manage the network of camps under their command.

Because something had to be done, the War Department established a top-secret organization called the Prisoner of War Special Projects Division (SPD). Under the aegis of SPD, educators and political scientists, all experts in the nuances of Nazi Germany, were assembled in Washington to design and launch an elaborate plan for reeducating and reprogramming German POWs.

Intellectual Diversion Program (IDP)

The first objective of the plan was to change the attitude of the average German POW toward American democracy and thereby lessen the influence of Nazism in the camps. Success here promised to make the Army's prisoner management job easier.

The second was to create a cadre of democratic thinkers among the POWs who would assume positions of leadership in the new German government after the War ended. Success here would influence Germany's transition from a culture highly susceptible to totalitarianism to a culture highly resistant to any form of government other than democracy.

In its wisdom, the Pentagon chose a palatable name for its plan to reeducate and reprogram Nazi-brainwashed POWs. It was known as the Intellectual Diversion Program or IDP. The Program was launched in 1944.

Most German POWs had never been exposed to American or British literature or arts. Under IDP, prisoners were provided with German-language versions of the works of authors such as John Steinbeck, Robert Louis Stevenson, and Mark Twain. American magazines and newspapers were distributed in POW camps. American and British movies, dubbed in German when possible, were shown regularly.

Community work programs enabled POWs to labor side by side with ordinary Americans and to visit farms and other places of business where they could see for themselves the products and the power of American capitalism and democracy.

Classes were offered in American history and political science. Later, vocational specialties were added to the curriculum, including auto repair, electric power, and horticulture.

POWs were given the opportunity to earn academic degrees by enrolling in courses taught at the camps by faculty members from nearby universities and colleges. This particular aspect of IDP was extremely popular among the Germans, who placed a high value on academic achievement.

Under the terms of an agreement negotiated by the International Red Cross in Switzerland, German POWs in America could take college courses taught by American professors and receive credits granted by German universities. And, similarly, American POWs in Germany took courses taught by German professors for credits granted by American colleges.

Many German POWs earned their degrees in subjects that would make them influential when they returned to Germany after the War ended. The most popular courses were those leading to a degree in education. Attesting to the success of the IDP, a rather high proportion of former POWs ultimately filled positions of importance in Germany's post-War government in Bonn.

The same was true for American POWs who enrolled in classes while serving as POWs in Europe. Most notable was Nicholas Katzenbach, a future Attorney General of the United States.

Nicholas Katzenbach

Nickolas Katzenbach, a nineteen-year-old Princeton University student whose uncle was once mayor of Trenton, was fired up with patriotism when he heard the news of Pearl Harbor. In fact, he skipped his classes and drove to New York to enlist.

A month later, Katzenbach received a commission in the Army Air Force and said goodbye for four years to a life of comfort in one of Princeton's most prominent families. Trained as a navigator in B-25 bombers, Nick Katzenbach got his baptism of fire by flying missions over Italy and the Mediterranean Sea in support of the North African campaign. If he made it through his 19th bombing run on February 2, 1943, he would earn a period of rest care.

"We hit five Italian barges with six bombs. Then a destroyer hit us. Our left wing caught fire and we crashed into the sea at 270 miles per hour."

Katzenbach survived. But once he and his surviving crew got into a life raft, they were captured by an Italian seaplane.

The POWs ended up at Stalag Luft 3, near Sagan, Germany. It was later celebrated in the movie, *The Great Escape*, where about seventy-six American and British POWs staged a cunning tunnel breakout. Katzenbach did not join the escape, but he helped by hiding the excavated dirt.

The enemy within the POW compound was not the Germans and not the hunger, even though Katzenbach lost forty-five pounds off his six-foot-two, 205-pound frame. The enemy was boredom.

"It was just frustrating, but I had a way to deal with it, though. I said, I'll only be in prison for ninety days. When the ninety days were over, I'd say it again. And when those ninety days were over, I'd say it again. And eventually, I was right."

Katzenbach had another way to deal with the boredom. During his two years of captivity, he read 500 books supplied by the YWCA. These included works written by Plato, Shakespeare, Galsworthy, Locke, and Herodotus.

When he was finally liberated in March 1945, he didn't have to go back to college. Instead, he took his exams and was allowed to graduate. Then, he attended Yale Law School, where he was editor-in-chief of the *Yale Law Journal*. Katzenbach also received a Rhodes scholarship and studied at Oxford University for two years. In 1950, he became an attorney in New Jersey.

While serving as Attorney General of the United States under President Lyndon Johnson, he was a key figure in the civil rights struggle. It was he who delivered the order to integrate the University of Alabama. He also served as Deputy Secretary of State.

After leaving the government, he practiced law in Washington, D.C. and served as adviser to his son, John, who wrote a novel about life in a POW camp.

Katzenbach's story speaks to the success of the Intellectual Diversion Program. And there were many others!

Evaluating IDP

Historians disagree on whether the IDP program was a success or not. There were strong arguments on both sides of this question. Both sides, however, do agree that the IDP program did no harm.

One component of the program was viewed favorably by most everyone. POWs in America learned that if they cooperated by performing work on farms and in factories outside their camps, they would avoid being transferred to a special camp for Nazis, presumably as a form of punishment.

After the War, when the POWs left America to work for our European allies, many became disillusioned and embittered by their treatment there, including reduced food rations and additional years of forced labor rebuilding those countries.

However, one thing was certain, most POWs came to regard America as the bulwark against advances of the USSR into Europe. While POWs were not Americanized in this country nor in our European camps, they did recognize the United States as a potential ally against the political and economic challenges of the postwar world.

"The tragedy of this Sudeten woman, unable to conceal her misery as she dutifully salutes the triumphant Hitler, is the tragedy of the silent millions who have been `won over' to Hitlerism by the 'everlasting use' of ruthless force." *Photo from the National Archives. Identifier: 535891.*

Distribution of the major POW Base Camps POW in the United
States as of June 1944.
U.S. Army photo.

2. America Enters the POW Business

In 1945, the population of the United States was 140 million. Roughly 12% of all Americans fought in World War II. Nearly every family had one or more members fighting in the War.

Small towns across the country, such as Owosso, Michigan, Crossville, Tullahoma, and Clarksville, Tennessee - not far from Nashville - were among hundreds of American communities where permanent POW camps were established during World War II. (Appendix G: POW Camps in Tennessee.)

There were just a few POWs in America during World War I. However, when World War II ended, there were some 5,000 Japanese, 51,000 Italian, and 379,000 German POW for a total of 435,000 prisoners in America! And, at the end of the War, there was a huge additional number of POWs in our camps in both Europe and Asia.

Prelude to World War II

The following historical events culminated in the Japanese attack on Pearl Harbor on December 7, 1941. Then, the United States joined the Allies (Britain, France, and Russia) in fighting the Axis (Germany, Japan, and Italy) and provided detention facilities for POWs. (Appendix E: Strength of Allied and Axis Forces.)

January 30, 1933. Adolf Hitler becomes Chancellor of Germany. His Nazi Party, the Third Reich, takes power, and Hitler becomes the dictator of Germany.

October 25, 1936. Nazi Germany and Fascist Italy sign the Rome-Berlin Axis Treaty.

November 25, 1936. Nazi Germany and Imperial Japan sign the Anti-Comintern Pact, a pact against communism and Russia.

September 1, 1939. Nazi Germany invades Poland.

September 3, 1939. America's future allies, Britain and France, declare war on Nazi Germany.

April 9 to June 9, 1940. Nazi Germany invades and takes control of Denmark and Norway.

May 10 to June 22, 1940. Germany uses quick strikes, called Blitzkriegs, to take over much of Western Europe, including the Netherlands, Belgium, and Northern France.

May 30, 1940. Winston Churchill becomes leader of the British government.

June 10, 1940. Italy enters the War as a member of the Axis powers.

July 10, 1940. Germany launches air attacks on Great Britain. These attacks last until the end of October and are known as the Battle of Britain.

September 22, 1940. Germany and the Axis Powers attack Russia with a huge force of over four million troops.

December 7, 1941. The Japanese attack the U.S. Navy at Pearl Harbor. The next day, America enters World War II on the side of the Allies.

America Enters the POW Business

In 1943, we landed in North Africa, to join forces with the British who were fighting there against the Germans and the Italians. The British had no building materials to construct POW camps and couldn't spare the men to guard POWs. The United States was asked to take custody of 50,000 of their prisoners. This first POW contingent was shipped back to America on the empty Liberty ships that had just off-loaded American troops and equipment in Algeria and Morocco.

The first German POWs to dock in New York City were surprised to see the Statue of Liberty and the Manhattan skyline, because Nazi propaganda claimed those familiar sights had been flattened by the Luftwaffe's long-range bombers. In fact, Germany had no bombers capable of crossing the Atlantic Ocean.

The Allies defeated Rommel's Afrika Korps in North Africa in November 1943. This victory, along with successful campaigns across Sicily and up the boot of Italy, added substantially to the number of Germans to be shipped to America for imprisonment.

This was a critical issue, because there had been no preparation for facilities to house them. The primary focus was on the build-up of our Armed Forces after Pearl Harbor. But within weeks, the U.S. Provost Marshall General submitted a program of prison camp construction to the Joint Chiefs of Staff, proposing that these camps be built on American military bases having room to accommodate them and on the hundreds of abandoned Civilian Conservation Corps (CCC) camps.

These CCC camps were perfect for housing POWs. Originally, they were established to provide rural employment to the great number of unemployed young men during the Depression. The camps were constructed close to rural work projects located primarily in the South and Southwest far from the critical War industries in the Midwest and the East.

In addition, the War Department opened a number of military bases that had extra space to house the prisoners. Those bases included:

- Camp Forrest, Tennessee (3,000 POWs)
- Camp Clark, Missouri (3,000 POWs)
- Fort Bliss, Texas (1,350 POWs)
- Fort Bragg, North Carolina (1,680 POWs)
- Fort Devens, Massachusetts (1,000 POWs)
- Fort Meade, Maryland (1,680 POWs)
- Fort Oglethorpe, Georgia (948 POWs)
- Camp McCoy, Wisconsin (100 POWs)
- Fort Sam Houston, Texas (1,000 POWs)
- Camp Shelby, Mississippi (1,200 POWs)
- Fort Sill, Oklahoma (700 POWs)

Prison camps established at these locations used existing facilities when available. If not, camps were built from scratch.

To prevent mass escapes, prisoners were dispersed widely in 155 base camps and 785 branch camps located all over the country, ideally at least 170 miles from the coast and 150 miles from the Canadian and Mexican borders.

Base camps were located on 365 acres and housed from 2,000 to 4,000 POWs. The branch camps were located near farms and businesses where 435,000 POWs were employed. Branch camps typically housed a few hundred POWs.

As a rule, camps were not located near military bases, shipyards, or defense factories. Most were built in the South or Southwest because these regions offered isolation in addition to POW employment opportunities and, of course, a warmer climate to reduce heating costs.

These initial locations were estimated to satisfy about 75% of the immediate need for housing POWs.

To meet the need for housing the estimated additional 144,000 POWs who were arriving, $50 million was needed to acquire the land and to build the necessary additional camps.

The question became where and in what form would these additional camps be constructed?

American POW Camps

In constructing new camps, unlike our other Allies, England and the Soviet Union, we closely followed the guidelines spelled out in the Geneva Convention. Locations that did not have enough space for both prisoners and guards required both to live in tents.

Base camps consisted of the following facilities:

- Barracks for housing POWs and their Guards
- Mess halls
- Roadways covering the camp
- Cold storage facility
- Infirmary
- Dental clinic
- Fire station
- Post exchange
- Storehouse
- Prisoner guardhouse
- Chapel
- Showers and laundry facilities with hot and cold running water
- Soccer field
- Post office
- Warehouse
- Utility area
- Watch towers with searchlights
- Double chain link fences – ten feet high and eight feet apart.

The POW camps were elaborate and well-constructed. Many Americans considered them too grand for the POWs. It was said the many American communities referred to the camps outside of town as *The Fritz Ritz*.

All POW camps were isolated and as heavily guarded as possible. Thus, two-thirds of the camps, holding about three-fourths of the prisoners were located in the southern and southwestern regions of the United States. The rest of the camps were built throughout the eastern and western regions of the country.

By July of 1944 there were ninety-eight POW base camps across America. By the end of the War, this number had risen to 155 base camps.

Canadian POW Camps

There were forty POW camps across Canada during World War II, including camps that held Canadians of German and Japanese descent. Twenty-five camps exclusively held prisoners from foreign countries, nearly all from Germany.

At first, the camps were identified by letters and then by numbers. In addition to the base camps, there were branch camps and labor camps. The prisoners were used to perform various tasks. Many worked in forests as logging crews or on nearby farms. As in America, they were paid a nominal amount for their labor. Approximately 11,000 POWs were so employed by 1945.

Ultimately these camps held 33,798 prisoners, including both POWs and civilian internees.

As in America, POWs were protected by the conditions of the Geneva Convention. There were claims that conditions in the Canadian POW camps tended to be better than the conditions of the barracks of Canadian troops. POWs were guarded by the Veterans Guard of Canada, mostly men who had been soldiers during WW I.

Some believed that the lenient treatment foiled many escape attempts before they even started. Notably, it is told that a group of German prisoners returned to Camp Ozada after escaping, because the escapees encountered a Canadian phenomenon, a grizzly bear.

Beginning in 1945, all POWs were released and ultimately returned to their home countries. While none were allowed to remain in Canada, some returned later as immigrants.

Stalag: U.S.A.
by Judith M. Ginsberg

Today, few people realize that almost 380,000 German POWS in America were the subjects of a unique experiment in political reprogramming. In *Stalag: U.S.A.,* Judith Ginsberg details a top-secret, multimedia effort to combat Nazism the POW camps and to bring about a democratic appreciation among the prisoners. The War Department hoped this would not only change their views but would also provide a vanguard for redirecting postwar Germany.

Bedford Springs Hotel, from a circa mid-1920s postcard.

3. American Resorts Support the POW Program

During World War II, when the American resort industry basically evaporated, hotels served different functions for the United States government, including as internment facilities for the Axis (German, Italian, and Japanese) diplomats, interrogation centers, military schools, hospitals, rehabilitation facilities, and boot camps.

Sailors and Japanese Diplomats at the Bedford Springs Hotel

Bedford, Pennsylvania, was the location of the Bedford Springs Hotel, a summer resort with a 150-year history. However, from May 1941 until December 1944, the hotel was a Naval Radio Training School. Each class attended an intensive four-month course in radio communications. During this period, the school graduated over 7,000 Navy radiomen.

Bedford residents referred to school's students and instructors as the *Mountain Navy Men*. Civilian instructors for the naval school boarded in Bedford homes. On Saturday nights, Bedford citizens would observe the Navy enlisted men walking to town from the Springs hotel.

But toward the end of the War, these American military students of radio communication techniques were replaced by Japanese diplomats.

Following the departure of the Navy, the State Department leased the hotel as a residence for Japanese diplomats and their families who had been captured by the Allies in Germany. During the last days of the War, when the fall of Berlin was imminent, these Japanese, from their embassy in Berlin, fled to escape the approaching Allied forces. Denied entrance into Switzerland, they were taken into custody by the American 7th Army at Bad Gastein, an Austrian resort.

The diplomats included General Oshima, the Japanese ambassador to Germany, his military and technical advisors and their families, embassy staff members including cooks, chauffeurs, and maids, and even a contingent of Japanese businessmen and reporters. All were selected to be interned as POWs at the Bedford Springs Hotel.

Upon hearing the news of these expected new residents, Bedford citizens were outraged, because it was reported that many Bedford County servicemen were starving and being tortured in Japanese prison camps at that time. Local residents who worked at the hotel reluctantly provided services to the Japanese, who were enjoying their resort holiday. For security purposes, barbed-wire fences with guard towers enclosed the hotel and its surrounding lawns. This precaution was taken to prevent angry

Bedford residents from retaliating against the new Japanese hotel guests.

On August 8, 1945, two days following the atomic bombing of Hiroshima, the 147 Japanese detainees arrived at the Bedford Springs Hotel. On August 14th, Japan surrendered unconditionally, and World War II soon ended.

On this occasion, Bedford residents drove out of town, turned south on Route 220, passed the Bedford Springs Hotel, and then returned to town and repeated the circuit. Cars and trucks decorated in red, white and blue honked their horns. One car had a loudspeaker that played patriotic music. In a seemingly endless procession, celebrants continued the parade for hours, apparently to get the goat of the new and unwanted Japanese internees.

In mid-October, the State Department decided to transport these internees back to Japan as soon as transportation was available. On November 16, 1945, the Japanese departed and arrived in Seattle on November 20th to board a ship for Japan the following morning.

Luxury Hotels as Diplomatic Internment Centers

The Greenbriar Hotel and the Homestead Resort

Following the attack on Pearl Harbor on December 7, 1941, American law enforcement officers arrested diplomats of the Axis powers and charged them with being enemies of the United States. After questioning, these diplomats were moved away from Washington to secluded areas for their safety and to prevent them from leaking information to Axis agents.

Under the 1929 Geneva Convention, the U.S. was required to protect them and their families. The State Department contracted with two resorts. In May 1942, German diplomats and German news correspondents were relocated to the Greenbriar Hotel in White Sulphur Springs, West Virginia and the Japanese to the Homestead Hotel in Hot Springs, Virginia. These internment camps for enemy alien diplomats were luxurious, because we wanted our own diplomats in Berlin and Tokyo to be treated well.

These diplomats remained at these two resorts while the Allies and the Axis worked out the specifics for prisoner exchanges through the American Red Cross. Finally, the Japanese were moved into the Greenbriar to join their German counterparts. Schools were established at the Greenbriar for their children.

By December 1942, German and Japanese diplomats were moved to neutral countries in South America and Madagascar, as part of an exchange for captured American diplomats. The Greenbriar then transitioned into a hospital for injured American soldiers.

The Hershey Hotel

The Hershey Hotel was located in Hershey, Pennsylvania. On November 12, 1942, the Hershey's general manager, Joseph Gasslet, offered the hotel's facilities to the State Department as housing for the Vichy French diplomatic staff. Specifically, the offer was $7.50 per day to house adults and $4 for children and guards. The State Department would pay for incidental expenses and gratuities.

The first detainees included the Vichy French Ambassador Henry-Haye with seven members of his Washington D. C. staff and their families. Over ninety-four French citizens, designated as security risks, were interned at the Hershey Hotel. There they enjoyed golf, tennis, hotel amenities, and sprawling lawns enclosed by guard shacks and barbed-wire fence.

By September 1943, only the ambassador and sixteen others remained. Those with families agreed to work with the Allies and were released. The remaining Vichy detainees were moved to the Homestead Hotel in Warm Springs, Virginia. In October 1943, the Hershey Hotel reopened as a resort.

The Grove Park Inn

During the war, the Grove Park Inn in Asheville, North Carolina, was also used as an internment center for Axis diplomats. Diplomats and their staffs supported the local economy by purchasing goods from local merchants. Following their exchange for American diplomats, the Inn was leased by the U.S. Navy as a R&R (rest and rehabilitation) center. During 1944 and 1945, the hotel became an Army Redistribution Center where soldiers relaxed before moving to other duties. Then, the exiled Philippine Government functioned from the Presidential Cottage on the grounds of the Grove Park Inn.

Resorts as Interrogation Centers

Early in the War, the War Department realized that it needed special camps to interrogate certain POWs captured either by the Army or Navy.

Since the Geneva Convention prohibited setting up centers to interrogate prisoners, the American government copied the British and constructed centers to look like processing centers where POWS were housed before sending them to permanent, established camps. Rather than punishment, good living quarters, food, and recreational facilities encouraged prisoners to divulge information. Anti-Nazi Germans who worked for the American government mingled with the POWs and gained even more intelligence. These activities were kept secret from the civilian population and from the Swiss Government personnel who inspected the centers.

Two camps called *Interrogation Centers* were established at Fort Hunt near Alexandria, Virginia, and Camp Tracy at Byron Hot Springs Resort, located twenty miles west of Stockton, California. High-level officers, scientists, and political prisoners were sent to these camps. Fort Hunt was primarily for Germans and Italians.

Since few Japanese were taken prisoner until late in the War, Camp Tracy initially took the overflow from Fort Hunt. Later, Camp Tracy was divided into a German section and a Japanese section. During 1944, about 645 Germans and 921 Japanese prisoners were interrogated there, but there were only fifty-one prisoners at any one time. In each section, there were decoding rooms, maps drawn based on information received, and rooms where information was gathered by microphones hidden in the light fixtures in the prisoners' quarters. Wires were fed through the walls to the ground-level transcription room. In addition, prisoners' outdoor conversations were captured by listening devices in trees.

Intelligence did make a difference. Medical personnel revealed Japanese biological research. Naval personnel provided data about ships and their radar and armaments. Army POWs revealed code names for army units and locations of munitions plants.

Hotels as Hospitals and a Boot Camp

The Breakers in Palm Beach

Between 1942 and 1944, the War Department took over The Breakers in Palm Beach. The army operated it as Ream General Hospital, treating the wounded from the Allied invasion of North Africa. Under the command of the Medical Corps, 750 patients and 400 military staff lived there. Spaces served other purposes. The loggia was the officers' lounge. The ballroom became the recreation hall, and the mezzanine converted to operating rooms. The Coconut Grove Room transitioned into dental clinics. After the war, the hotel was restored.

The Palm Beach Biltmore Hotel

In June 1943, the Palm Beach Biltmore became the first school for the Coast Guard Women's Reserve (SPARS), created in 1942 to allow more men to be sent overseas. This six-week boot camp included courses in organization, personnel, ships, and aircraft. The women swabbed the hotel floors and had intense physical training at the Surf Club. After graduating, they were assigned to active duty or had more training to perform other duties as storekeepers, cooks, yeomen, stewards, bakers, pharmacist or dental mates.

Ahwahnee Hotel in Yosemite National Park, California

The Ahwahnee Hotel with its golf course, swimming pool, and tennis and croquet courts was a self-contained resort extremely costly to operate. In the summer of 1941, the Navy considered converting the Ahwahnee to a hospital. In 1943, the Navy leased the resort because of its remote location, the tranquility, and scenery. This facility, Yosemite Special Hospital, treated mentally traumatized sailors and marines.

Soon the Navy realized that the isolation was unbearable for shellshocked men. Lack of diversions produced boredom, and the cliffs produced claustrophobia. The hospital phased out its psychiatric treatment and converted the facility to a physical rehabilitation center. Improvements included a six-lane bowling alley, a library, a pool hall, basketball and tennis courts, a machine shop, a woodworking shop, a crafts center, and a store.

The hospital was decommissioned in December 1945. Today, it is a luxury hotel operated by the National Park Service.

The Ahwahnee Hotel, located in the center of the main valley of Yosemite National Park, was completed in 1927. The hotel features a unique blend of design influences including Art Deco, Native American, Middle Eastern and Arts & Crafts Movement. With its striking granite facade, magnificent log-beamed ceilings, massive stone hearths, and richly colored Native American artwork, the hotel is a National Historic Landmark. *Photo courtesy www.nps.gov. No protection is claimed in original U.S. Government works.*

"Thanks to my experience in Kansas and Oklahoma, I am an expert at harvesting broom corn and killing snakes."

Baron von Wechmar, a former German POW who became a member of the European Parliament.

4. POWs at Work in America

POWS Fill U.S. Labor Shortage

When the War began, America's population was 131 million. During the War, 16 million men and women, more than 12% of our population, served in the armed forces. Nearly half of American men between eighteen and forty were in uniform. At the same time, demand for workers in our booming war industry was never so great. Many of these positions were filled by women, who by all accounts, performed extremely well.

Fortunately, the Geneva Convention authorized the United States to compel POW enlisted men and non-commissioned officers to work as well. But that work could not be demeaning, dangerous or defense-related. Prisoners worked the same hours as their American counterparts, eight hours a day and six days a week, in jobs such as farming, forestry, and food processing. They were compensated for their work.

Before the War, the prisoners held a wide range of occupations. While most were common laborers, others were professionals, including doctors, dentists, and lawyers. But as POWs, they all were employed as common laborers regardless of their skills, knowledge, or experience. This might have been a waste of specialized skills, but it made the job of managing POWs simpler and easier.

POWs were often transported to camps on civilian passenger trains equipped with Pullman cars, enabling them to sleep comfortably. Ironically, their American guards were required to sleep in their seats on the train. While POWs were entitled to three meals a day from the dining car, their guards were only authorized to order two meals a day. These practices reinforced the attitude that the POWs were coddled.

POW Daily Routine

The daily schedules in all POW camps were nearly identical. Reveille took place at 5:30 am. Bunks were made, and prisoners were ready for breakfast by 6:00. By 6:30 the POWs had finished and were marched back to their barracks to shave and shower, clean the barracks, and police the area.

At 7:30, POWs began their work projects in camp or boarded trucks to be taken to nearby farms and factories to work. At noon, the POWs generally ate sack lunches out in the fields with their backs propped up against trees. At about 4:30 in the afternoon, farmers or factory supervisors began to gather the POWs' tools, and the POWs were loaded back into their trucks for the trip back to camp.

Following a shower and a change of clothes, usually into their German uniforms, the POWs ate dinner between 6:00 and 7:00, after which the evening was at their disposal.

POW Work Compensation

To reduce transportation costs and time, POW camps were located close to where POWs worked. Also, many camps were established in the South to reduce heating costs. Businesses or individuals, like farmers, contracted directly with the Army for POW laborers. They paid the prevailing labor rate, which back then averaged fifty-two cents an hour or about $4 a day.

Out of the $4, the POW's share was 80 cents a day plus a 10-cent daily allowance for personal items. The rest of the $4 went to the U.S. government to pay for housing the prisoners and to finance the War effort. The POW's 90-cent daily wage was approximately equal to the pay of a U. S. Army private during the War.

Half of a POW's pay (45 cents) was deposited in a savings account that the POW took home with him after his repatriation. The other 45 cents were paid in the form of canteen coupons. These coupons were used instead of cash to prevent POWs from accumulating money to finance an escape attempt.

Camp canteens operated by POWs sold:

- Cigarettes
- Pipe tobacco
- Soft drinks
- Ice cream
- Candy
- Beer and wine

POWs could even order items from the Sears Roebuck catalog using canteen coupons. Can't you just imagine a POW ordering a deer rifle?

POWs on American Farms

Most German POWs cherished their time spent in America during the War. This was particularly true of those who worked on American farms. Although fraternization was supposedly not allowed, farmers generally ignored the rule, plying hardworking POWs with tobacco, beer, wine, and extra food. No one was there to object, because small details of three to five POWs were assigned, without guards, to area farms.

In most cases, they ate at the dinner table with the farmer's family and other workers. They slept in makeshift bunkrooms in barns. The POW details were dropped off at the farms early Monday morning and picked up on Saturday afternoon.

When the War ended, both the POWs and the farm families were saddened when they parted. After the War, farmers sent gifts of much-needed foodstuffs and warm clothing to the POWs and their families. For decades after the War, they visited them in Europe.

POW Work Uniforms

POWs were allowed to retain their uniforms, which they wore during their leisure time. To perform work in the community outside the camp, all POWs were issued the same uniform: olive drab work pants, jacket, and billed cap, the same uniform worn by American soldiers assigned to KP duty. There was one clear difference. Five-inch, block letters **PW** were stenciled in bold, white dye on both sides of each pant leg. And, on the front and back of their work jackets, the **PW** symbol stood out, so you couldn't miss it, even at a great distance.

In addition to their work clothes, each POW was issued:

- 1 belt
- 2 pair of cotton trousers
- 2 pair of wool trousers
- 1 pair of gloves
- 1 wool coat
- 1 overcoat
- 1 pair of shoes
- 4 pair of socks
- 4 pair of undershorts
- 4 undershirts
- 1 raincoat
- 1 wool suit

Like their SS colleagues, the Afrika Korps SS soldiers were exceptionally vain. When captured and becoming POWs, they refused to wear the American standard army-issue work shoes worn by other POWs. They insisted on keeping their highly polished black leather boots. They maintained this refusal until performing their required POW labor in their stocking feet resulted in quickly lowering their standards.

POW Camp Food

In American camps, German POWs ate very well, especially compared to those Germans back in Europe in the army or on the home front. Some of the first POWs to arrive in America were soldiers from General Erwin Rommel's Afrika Korps. These tough fighters had survived on meager rations. Until they became accustomed to the large quantities of rich food served in POW camps, most became ill.

Schutzstaffel or SS translates as Protective Echelon. Initially, the SS served as Nazi Party leader, Adolf Hitler's, personal bodyguards and later became one of the most powerful and feared military organizations in all of Nazi Germany. Many SS also served with Rommel in Afrika.

POWs in America gained weight while in captivity. But American POWs in Axis camps experienced just the opposite. There were 94,000 American POWs in German prison camps. And there were 34,000 Americans in Japanese prison camps during the War.

The German POWs enjoyed an abundance of food, including delicacies they hadn't seen in years like coffee, eggs, and meat. Local American suppliers provided POW camps with high-quality meat, groceries, and produce. Ironically, at the same time, American citizens were deprived of these same items because of wartime rationing.

The experienced cooks among the POWs prepared food European-style to appeal to German tastes, so the prisoners would eat more and waste less. POWs told the German Red Cross to discontinue sending food items to America and, instead, distribute them to German citizens on the German home front. These food items just weren't needed in American POW camps.

Some Germans' food preferences seemed odd to Americans. Instead of butter, they preferred chopped onions and lard on bread.

In Germany, field corn was grown only as feed for livestock. So, POWs reaction to sweet corn was *Das ist fir Schwein!* That's for pigs! But after the first taste of fresh sweet corn, their objections disappeared.

A typical POW standard menu included:

Breakfast

Corn Flakes
Cake or Bread with Marmalade
Coffee or Milk
Sugar

Lunch

Roast Pork
Potato Salad - Carrots
Ice Water

Supper

Meat Loaf
Scrambled or Boiled Eggs
Coffee or Milk
Bread

When learning of the POW menus, returning American soldiers were incensed that they had been forced to survive on meager C-rations or K-rations while fighting on the front lines. These complaints were acknowledged, but little, if anything, was done to modify the POWs' diet. Military officials were convinced that well-fed German POWs were docile and content and not likely to cause trouble or to attempt to escape.

Guests Behind the Barbed Wire
German POWS in America: A True Story of Hope and Friendship
by Ruth Beaumont Cook

In *Guests behind the Barbed Wire,* Ruth Beaumont Cook chronicles the building and operation of the largest German POW camp in the United States during World War II. It presents in meticulous detail how the residents of Aliceville, Alabama, helped build, operate, and supply the camp, and then become intertwined with camp life and the 6,000 German POWS held there.

Sports was the most popular pastime in POW camps in America with organized teams and uniforms at many camps. Americans attended these games, cheering for their favorite POWs. Above is the starting eleven of the German POW soccer team from the camp at Roswell, NM. *Photo courtesy of James A. Downey.*

5. POWs' Leisure Time

POW Recreational Activities

Rather than have POWs obsessively preoccupied with their fate as prisoners, studies showed great benefits of providing POWs with a variety of diversions to occupy their time and minds.

A variety of camp activities were offered by camp commanders. But POWs' choices depended greatly on their own interests.

Sports was definitely the most popular pastime. Soccer, called *football* by the Germans, was universally enjoyed by nearly every German or Italian POW. Germans also liked to play *fistball*, volley ball to us.

Arnold Kramer's *Nazi Prisoners of War in America*, contains the following quote from Alfred Klein, a German POW interned in Camp Opelika, Alabama. Klein recalls:

"Our camp had a whole slate of outstanding teams in soccer, handball, volleyball, etc. The Camp Championships, especially in soccer and handball, were so exciting that even our guards participated as cheerleaders from their towers and attended the

games on weekends with their own families, shouting from the sidelines. Many of our athletes, as a matter of fact, went on to professional sports careers in Germany after the War."

The YMCA donated the balls and other sports equipment, as well as other recreational items, including books, musical instruments, phonograph records, games, and hobby materials.

<u>Plays and theatrical productions</u> were the second most popular pastime. Every camp had a makeshift theater, usually at one end of the mess hall, in which POWs performed everything from uproariously funny skits to highly sophisticated three-act plays with props and orchestration.

<u>Choral groups and orchestras</u> were organized. Instruments were donated by organizations and individuals in cities where the camps were located.

<u>Classes to earn college credit</u> were offered. In their leisure time, POWs attended courses accepted by nineteen universities in Germany and Austria. These courses were taught by local American college professors. Credit hours were recorded in a logbook prepared by the German High Command just at the time when Germany was losing badly on the Russian front and the Allies were poised to invade Normandy.

<u>Church services</u> were provided on Sundays by the local churches, sometimes in German. Prisoners were either transported to churches or, in some cases, local ministers came to the camps. Many camps provided German hymnals. But POWs had to break a bad hymn-singing habit. Back in Germany, Nazi leaders had ordered them to substitute the word *Hitler* for the word *God* when they sang hymns. When that nonsense stopped, most POWs seemed relieved.

<u>Tracking down distant relatives</u> in America became a major activity for many German POWs. The POWs even had visiting hours at the camps. They could see visitors once a month for a one-hour period. Their American relatives would drive great distances to be at the camp for only an hour. That's not much time, so some visited their POWs on the farms where they worked, bringing them treats that the POWs smuggled back into camp.

<u>Marriage</u>. Most POWs were unmarried - only about one in ten was married. Europeans tended to marry at older ages, and most POWs were in their early twenties. Some were only teenagers. Nonetheless, there were budding romances. POWs were allowed to send a single postcard each week and a single, short letter the next. Even at this rate, they seemed to be able to start and maintain long-distance romances. This correspondence often resulted in the desire to tie the knot, and POWs were able to marry their sweethearts back home - by proxy.

Weddings were arranged through the International Red Cross and conducted by local clergy, including cake, flowers, and best man. But no bride. After the ceremony was conducted in the camp, the paperwork was sent off to Germany through the Red Cross. The weddings were perfectly legal.

<u>Newspapers</u>. Sometimes, POWs published their own newspapers.

<u>Movies</u>. POWs liked English language movies, especially the propaganda films like *Why We Fight* and anti-Nazi movies like *Watch on the Rhine*. Periodically, the projector was turned off so a translator could explain what was happening.

<u>Pets</u> were popular. In the camps, POWs had pets including cats, dogs, monkeys, and canaries.

Contraband, for the most part, was harmless. Candy, tobacco, and so on. But one of the POW cooks at Camp Owosso had an old uncle, from Pinconning, who'd visit about once a month. After the uncle's visit, the cook always ended up drunk. It took the guards awhile to figure out that the uncle hid a bottle of liquor in the weeds near the garbage pit before he went through the normal visitor's search. Later, when the cook went out to empty the kitchen garbage, he'd retrieve the bottle and have himself a party. The camp guards soon put an end to it.

Freedom for Some. After Mussolini's defeat in 1943, Italian POWs in America had permission to take sightseeing trips and attend dances and dinners in local Italian communities. They worked paying jobs on military bases and in government buildings.

German POWs Entertained by Lena Horne

In the 1930s, after a turbulent youth, Lena Horne moved to New York City where she worked as a chorus-line girl in Harlem's famous *Cotton Club*. Although gaining entrance to professional singing proved difficult for her, she became the first African-American to tour with an all-white band in 1940. After entering a film career as a singer and touring to promote her films, she became one of the top night club and theater attractions in the United States.

During World War II, when entertaining the troops for the USO, she refused to perform her show when she realized that her audience was configured as follows:

- In the front seats, U.S. white soldiers.
- Next, German white soldiers.
- In the back seats, U.S. black soldiers.

Observing that the black soldiers had been forced to sit in the back seats, she walked off the stage to the first row of black troops and performed with Germans and white soldiers behind her. After quitting the USO in 1945 because of the organization's policy of segregating audiences, Horne self-financed tours of military camps.

High-Ranking German Officers as POWs

During the War, forty German generals and two admirals were interned in American POW camps. By design, they were treated with great deference because of their likely influence in Germany after the War. Retired American officers of the same rank were assigned as their liaison officers and guides. These Americans were all graduates of West Point and Annapolis, which insured they were well-versed in the nuances of military tradition and courtesy.

These high-ranking German officers were taken on tours of shipyards and war plants to impress them with the size and vitality of the American war machine.

All German officers regardless of rank were given radios to listen to whatever they wished. They were amazed at the openness of the news in America.

The officers' spacious quarters, with gardens, were sumptuous, a minimum of 120 square feet of living space for officers compared to 40 square feet for enlisted POWs.

German officers were not required to work. Instead they were assigned personal drivers and automobiles and encouraged to roam freely within a radius of 50 miles from their camps. They were bound only by their word of honor not to attempt to escape. And not one ever broke his word.

Officers had full pay and benefits. Personal chefs prepared their meals, and servants kept their quarters in impeccable condition. In short, these were far better conditions than they would have experienced fighting the Russians on the Eastern front. In fact, German Officer POWs fared far better in the United States than their American counterparts in German camps.

Remarkably, five hardened German submarine officers were allowed to travel *unescorted* together on a train to their new POW camp, Camp Blanding, Florida. They had no dress uniforms for the trip, so they were allowed to wear the uniform of a U.S. Naval officer with one exception. They wore small Nazi lapel pins so they couldn't be accused of being spies. During their trip, there were no problems from the five or from Americans along the way.

Coddling Charges

Naturally, some Americans accused the military of coddling the POWs, but the War Department refuted the charge by citing these benefits. First, when word of our generous treatment of POWs reached the German army, it would encourage more of them to surrender and thus shorten the War. Second, such treatment made for docile POWs who required fewer guards. This meant more American soldiers could be sent to the front lines. And third, the POWs were more cooperative and worked harder at their jobs, thus helping in the War effort.

Though it may be hard to believe, serious consideration was given to a top-secret proposal to allow POWs to transfer to the U.S. Army as the *German Volunteer Corps* to fight against the Japanese in the Pacific.

In appreciation for the sincere hospitality of their American hosts, some POWs donated their savings accounts to local Community Chest campaigns when they were repatriated.

POW Reaction to Life in America

For millions of Americans, especially farmers and owners of small businesses, the availability of German POWs employed as workers was a lifesaver. Likewise, for German POWs spending their War years in America, even as POWs, this was a dream come true. They were treated far better here in our country than they had ever experienced in the German armed forces.

In general, enlisted German POWs were also content with their lives as residents of American POW camps. After all, they spent their time usefully, working for American businesses or on farms and were paid for their services. They enjoyed wholesome meals, prepared especially for them by farmers' wives or business cafeterias.

Without exception, enlisted POWs gained weight, maintained healthy bodies, and relaxed in their new lifestyles as POWs in America. The vast majority of German POWs cherished their time spent here. This was particular true of those who worked on American farms.

A survey was sent to each repatriated POW. Three quarters of them expressed appreciation and thanks to their American captors or, as most Germans viewed them, their *hosts*. Appropriately 5,000 former German POWs immigrated to America between 1948 and 1960. The tightness of immigration standards on the millions who wanted to immigrate here greatly reduced the number.

German POW Re-education Programs

As American leaders realized the War in Europe was coming to an end, there was a great concern about the fate of postwar Germany. Our leaders were concerned about the uncertainty of Germany's future ideology. Would Germany's fascism be supplanted by communism? By a return of the monarchy? Or, as we hoped, by democracy?

After all, we had invested in fighting. Now it seemed certain that in winning this terribly costly War, the worst possible outcome would be that Germany's Nazi ideology would remain the same and its population would be unrepentant.

After our gigantic investment of money and lives expended to win the war with Germany, something simply *had* to be done to alter this possible outcome.

On occasion, prison officials experienced the Nazis' conditioning. When digging drain ditches in America, POWs found some Indian arrowheads and asked the guard where they should turn them in. In Nazi Germany, all artifacts like those belonged to the State. The guard advised them to keep the arrowheads and show them to their grandchildren.

Author's Note. One morning, I observed an amusing incident on Corunna Avenue in my hometown, Owosso, Michigan. An army truck loaded with POWs slowed down before turning into the canning factory. A gang of six-year-old boys ran alongside the truck yelling, "Hello, Hitler!" The POWs laughed, waved back, and returned the kids' Nazi salutes, to the delight of the boys.

The Army established a Special Projects Division (SPD), which was responsible for educating German POWs on the American way of life. To spread the word, some eighty POW camp newspapers were launched. Also, a national, bi-monthly POW newspaper-magazine was created, called *Der Ruf (The Call)*. By October 1945, Der Ruf had a circulation of 75,000. Each sold for five cents and was very popular among the German POWs.

In early May 1945, the Special Projects Division launched the Intellectual Diversion Program (IDP) to promulgate movies to POWs that featured American War heroes and documented Nazi atrocities. The movie attendance was relatively high. The cost of admission was 25 cents. A total of 8,243,635 admissions were sold, meaning that each POW, on average, watched thirty movies. Since movie dialog was in English, frequently the movie was stopped to allow for translation into German.

Between October 1944 and February 1945, church attendance rose to 30% of the POW population.

As mentioned earlier, POWs volunteered to serve in the U.S. Army fighting the Japanese in the Pacific, but that was turned down. However, 3,700 German POWs were specially trained to be German police officers serving with the American occupation forces after the War.

Just before being repatriated to Germany to work with American occupation forces, 23,147 German POWs attended crash courses on democracy. The remaining POWs were repatriated to other Allied countries. Their purpose was to help those countries repair the extensive damages that Nazi Germany had inflicted on them.

America Exits the POW Business

Why do so few people today know about POWs in America during

WWII? There are two reasons. First, by 1946, every POW had left America, but they were not *repatriated*. Our German POWs were handed over to our European allies who put them to work rebuilding those countries that the Nazis had crushed with their bombs and artillery fire during the War.

They were distributed and employed as follows: France took 200,000 to work on French farms, mines, and in construction and forestry jobs. Britain took 175,000 to clear rubble, mine coal, and perform various jobs for the air ministry. Belgium accepted 40,000 for reconstruction jobs. The Netherlands, Scandinavia, Czechoslovakia, Yugoslavia, and Greece accepted a total of 20,000 to meet their needs. These POWs worked with our Allies until 1949 or 1950 before they were allowed to return to their German homeland. So, technically, that was when they were finally repatriated.

"At Camp Carson, Colorado, the prisoners created a bit of the Fatherland by building an authentic beer garden for use during their off hours. The beer garden was complete with chairs, tables, and decorations made in the camp woodcraft shop. With this beer garden, indoor and outdoor sports, woodworking shop, theater, school classes, camp newspaper, and plays, Camp Commander, Lieutenant General Eugene N. Frakes, was able to report: 'Morale is unbelievably high.' "

From *Nazi Prisoners of War in America* by Arnold Krammer.

The Army established a POW branch camp on the former Civilian Conservation Corps (CCC) campgrounds near the intersection of M-21 and Carland Road about five miles west of Owosso. *Photo courtesy of Linda Ruehle.*

6. Camp Owosso

During World War II, over 6,000 prisoners were housed in POW camps in Michigan. Approximately 1,000 POWs were held in the Upper Peninsula. In the Lower Peninsula, 5,000 POWs were housed in thirty-two camps. (See Appendix H: POW Camps in Michigan.)

Many of the camps were former Civilian Conservation Corps (CCC) barracks, unused since that program was discontinued in 1942. Most of our first POWs were German soldiers captured in North Africa. We had agreed to accept 50,000 POWs from the British after we joined their fight against the Germans and Italians in 1942.

World War II created a huge labor shortage in the United States due to the draft. One solution was to use POW labor in the agriculture and forestry fields. Approximately 60% of the POWs in Michigan were contracted out to work on farms, growing and harvesting fruit and other crops. POWs also cut pulpwood in forests of the Upper Peninsula.

Mexican and Jamaican Workers during the War

Shipments of sugar from South America and the Caribbean were curtailed by the presence of German U-boats. So, America replaced cane sugar with beet sugar, much of which was grown on Michigan farms, including those around Owosso.

During the War, in addition to POWs, Owosso was home to many Mexican and Jamaican farm laborers. They worked in great numbers alongside POWs from Camp Owosso.

Farmers required workers to plant, weed, and harvest sugar beets by hand. They preferred the hard-working Mexican men, women, and children for these tasks. But during the War, they increased their harvests of sugar beets with the help of Jamaicans and German POWs from Camp Owosso.

Origin of Camp Owosso

In 1944, Michigan had a POW base camp at Fort Custer and thirty-two POW branch camps located throughout the state. At that time, the Army established a branch camp on the former Civilian Conservation Corps (CCC) campgrounds near the intersection of M-21 and Carland Road about five miles west of Owosso.

During the Great Depression, the camp had served as home to hundreds of CCC workers. CCC, part of President Roosevelt's *New Deal,* provided jobs related to conservation and development of natural resources on land owned by federal, state, and local governments.

To be eligible to work, CCC applicants had to be men who were unemployed, unmarried, and between the ages of eighteen and twenty-five. Some 2.5 million American men worked in CCC jobs over the course of the program's existence between 1933 and 1942.

When the CCC camps were closed, their facilities were relatively new. With a few shingles and a new coat of paint, many former CCC camps were quickly converted to POW camps. This provided a substantial savings of American taxpayer dollars.

Because of its proximity to my hometown, the Army named the POW camp, Camp Owosso. The fenced-in compound consisted of rows of tents, each housing six German POWs.

Gary Marsh, an Ortonville, Michigan resident, serving in the Fifth Armored Division, was one of the guards at Camp Owosso. In his interview with *The Citizen Online,* he said:

"I spent some of the time in the guard tower watching over about 400 prisoners. Some were Gestapo, the German secret state police. There were some tough Germans in that camp. Many of them were not Nazis, but they had been forced to fight in Hitler's army against their will.

"Some wanted to go home to Germany, but for the most part they never tried to run away from camp. They really liked it there. As a matter of fact, toward the end, the Army took away our ammunition when we were guarding the POWs. I guess they figured no one would get hurt if there were no bullets."

According to Greg Summer, a noted author on the subject of Michigan POW camps:

"The story of 6,000 German POWs, who were brought to Michigan beginning in 1943, is little remembered today. They lived in camps

scattered around the state and helped fill the labor gap, especially in agriculture. The bad guys, the hardcore Nazis and Fascist bullies, were weeded out, leaving mostly well-behaved, homesick young men held in minimum security facilities.

"The best part for me, is that, despite official rules against fraternization, many POWs established enduring friendships with the Americans they worked for. And many later returned to pursue a U.S. citizenship."

At the end of the War, the prisoners left America. But, as you read earlier, they did not go directly home. And postwar quotas set for German immigrants to America were extremely low. Only about 5,000 of the 379,000 German POWs in America during the War were eventually granted U.S. citizenship.

Owosso Citizens' Initial Reaction to Camp Owosso

At first, no one in Owosso considered having a POW camp named after the town a great honor. During the year the camp opened, an alarming number of Owosso's young men had returned home from North Africa or the Pacific with missing limbs or horrid burns, without sight, or *asleep* in wooden caskets. This unanticipated consequence from the patriotic rush to enlist immediately following Pearl Harbor generated powerful feelings of hatred toward America's enemies, especially the *Krauts and Japs* as they were commonly referred to.

Measured against today's standards, America during the War was a hotbed of intolerance. These labels, and some even worse, were used without restraint by politicians of both major parties, teachers, ministers, newspaper reporters, movie heroes, radio broadcasters, and the U.S. Government on propaganda posters prominently displayed on bulletin boards at post offices, in our factories, and at our schools.

This was the mood of our community when Camp Owosso's first POWs arrived. The reception was far from friendly. Too many Gold Stars were hung in windows by mournful mothers, like our next-door neighbor, Mrs. Mrva, who had lost two sons fighting the Germans in North Africa.

Could we engender even a modicum of Christian forgiveness, let alone hospitality, toward these unwanted Nazis in our midst? But we were human, too. We couldn't control our curiosity. We were a paradoxical muddle of childlike inquisitiveness wrapped in simmering hatred.

Most of the POWs at Camp Owosso in 1944 had been captured in North Africa. By 1945, a number of additional German POWs from the European theater, particularly Italy, were also housed there. While the camp population peaked to well over 1,000 in the summer months, the camp was not maintained during the winter.

Camp Owosso's POWs were either sent south to Fort Custer, a POW base camp located near Battle Creek, Michigan, or to northern Michigan where they lived in heated barracks and worked harvesting lumber from the forest-covered land. The exact number of POWs at Camp Owosso at any time was hard to calculate, because all POW records were returned to Germany, and the local camp administrative records were disposed of in the 1950s.

But as you read above and will read further in this book, attitudes relating to the POWs changed to positive as Owosso citizens' experiences over time proved them worthy of our admiration and respect.

Arrival of First POWs in Owosso

Fortunately for our community, a few weeks after the arrival of the POWs, Camp Owosso officials offered the townspeople an opportunity to use POWs to work in factories and on nearby farms. Our community leaders were told that the Geneva Convention permitted prisoners of war to work, providing their employers did not manufacture war materials and the POWs were compensated for their work.

Not surprisingly, because of labor shortages, our community leaders embraced the idea. The *Owosso Argus-Press* ran enticing articles encouraging POW utilization. The camp's Commanding Officer Captain Ohrt gave his sales pitch to responsive audiences at the Owosso City Council meeting and at the local Rotary and Kiwanis Clubs. The colonel even spoke on the subject at the Shiawassee Grange Hall before a full house of interested, but wary, Farm Bureau members.

Farm and factory workers were as scarce as hens' teeth at the height of the War. Many Owosso citizens not in the Armed Forces worked two or more jobs during that time.

So, eventually, farmers and local businessmen concluded that, rather than leave crops unharvested in fields or production lines sitting idle on off-shifts, they would accept the alternative of inexpensive and reliable POW labor. In short, this became a quintessential mutually beneficial relationship.

When the first allotment of POWs arrived at Camp Owosso, as I mentioned above, the citizens' reception was far from hospitable. But, if anything, back in those days Owossoites were pragmatic and extremely curious about our new German *guests*.

Shortly after the arrival of that first POW contingent, Owosso residents just had to see them – up close. They drove out to Camp Owosso, stopped their cars on the road that ran alongside the camp, and stared at the hundreds of German POWs a mere 100 feet away behind a double, high chain-link fence topped with barbed wire.

The Army engineers had clear-cut a wide swath around the perimeter of the camp to provide an open field of fire for the Army Military Police, the MPs, who manned the search lights and .50 caliber machine guns positioned atop the watch towers rising from the four corners of the compound.

Owosso visitors could clearly see the POWs, who stared back at them silently. This was an unsettling experience, as if we had intruded on something very private and sad. Visitors didn't stay long and were very moved by what they had observed.

Owosso residents watched intently as POWs traveled in the Army trucks on their way to work at nearby factories and farms. At the canning factory, POWs unloaded trucks of produce and carried it into the factory.

Ironically, people in Owosso soon discovered that the POWs were quite ordinary and normal. They laughed and poked fun at each other. They were cheerful and even friendly. Most of them were just young men, many only teenagers.

Owosso residents experienced mixed emotions regarding the POWs. This was not what they expected from the Nazis in their midst. Were these the *monsters* we were taught to hate by the newsreels, newspapers, and radio? Frankly, I liked what I saw but felt guilty. The more I observed the POWs, the more confused I became.

However, one thing prevented us from forgetting that these men were the enemy - Nazi soldiers! POWs were guarded by Army MPs with .45 automatics on their belts and Tommy guns in the crook of their arms. Despite our increasing familiarity with our POW neighbors, we never lost sight of the fact that this was serious business and these were serious times.

Incidentally, the Tommy gun was officially the Thompson submachine gun. This gun was invented by John T. Thompson in 1918. It became infamous during the Prohibition era as the signature weapon of various organized crime syndicates in the United States. The Tommy gun's rate of fire was approximately 600-725 rounds per minute. It fired .45 caliber cartridges and was an official U.S. Military weapon between 1938 and 1971.

POWs at the Canning Factory

During the workweek, from Monday through Saturday, POWs were transported with their armed guards in Army trucks to the W.R. Roach, a large canning factory in my old neighborhood. When their trucks stopped at the canning factory, the POWs dismounted, formed in rank, and marched into the factory, singing march songs to keep in step. German soldiers never called cadence. We Owosso kids were absolutely mesmerized by this remarkable daily occurrence.

We altered our route to Washington Elementary School each day. By walking through the canning factory parking lot, we could closely examine the POWs at work. We watched the POWs as they unloaded vegetables and fruits to be processed, canned, and sold to grocery distributors throughout Michigan.

The POWs seemed to be as interested in us, as we were interested in them. After a few days of watching us kids observe them unloading the trucks, POWs began to count on our being there. When we arrived, we were greeted by wide grins and friendly waves of welcome. This reaction warmed our hearts and created an even more passionate interest in the young, handsome, blond-haired POWs who appeared to be seeking our approval and friendship.

In a *Flint Journal* newspaper article written in 1944, a top manager shared remarks about the POWs working at the canning factory.

"At first we experienced a little difficulty. We didn't know how to handle them, because we spoke different languages. But after we got things straightened out, everything worked just fine. We couldn't have operated if it had not been for the services of these prisoners. At the peak of our operation, 95 percent of our male help were prisoners."

Michigan farmers and food processors employed between 4,000 and 5,000 POWs in 1944 and 1945.

Workers, POWs and civilian women, manned positions beside conveyer belts, carrying the fruit and vegetables from station to station. These foods were cleaned, cooked, pared into small pieces, and packed into tins or glass jars. Then, the appropriate label was pasted onto the side of each can or jar. Finally, the tins or jars were packed in cardboard boxes and shipped by rail to grocery distributors throughout Michigan.

During the War, factories in Owosso and around the country operated six days a week. Because most parents worked on Saturday, kids were free to spend the day with their friends. Many times, we spent the day at the canning factory watching the canning process being carried out by the POWs.

POWs were residents of Camp Owosso from mid-1944 until early 1946. When they departed for additional years of work in England and France after the War ended, many Owosso residents, including me, were saddened to see our *friends* depart.

POW Escape from Camp Owosso

After work on July 20, 1944, two teenage girls, Kitty Marie Case and Shirley Ann Druce, drove away from the canning factory in Owosso with two of their POW co-workers.

This was not a typical trip for refreshments from the local soda shop or to a dance pavilion. On the contrary, this was a jail break of sorts. More importantly, unknown to the two young women, their decision to drive away with their two German co-workers was a most serious crime that would cost them dearly in the very near future.

Their co-workers were Gottfried Hobel and Eric Classen. Both had recently served as soldiers in Nazi Germany's army before being captured and brought to the United States to serve their POW sentences in Camp Owosso.

Apparently the two young girls and their POW pals, after stopping off in Owosso's West Town to purchase several bottles of wine, decided to spend the night in the woods near Colby Lake in nearby Woodhull Township. But, thankfully, by the very next morning, our capable sheriff had captured all four fugitives.

Well actually, Sherriff Ray Gellatly and his deputy found them fast asleep where the couples had spent the night with the several bottles of wine. Evidently their intentions were not so much menacing as they were, shall we say, *romantic* in nature.

The POWs were returned to their camp and mildly disciplined. The two young women were scolded by the sheriff and then released. A photo in the next afternoon's Owosso *Argus-Press* showed the women with broad grins on their faces as they left the sheriff's office for home. That photo enraged Owosso's citizens, many of whom felt that the two irresponsible young women deserved the death penalty.

Moreover, after seeing the photo of the two grinning young women, FBI agents from the Detroit Field Office were hardly amused. Within hours, they rearrested the women and charged them with *treason*! This being wartime, if convicted, the women faced the death penalty.

News of the escape and trial made headlines all over the country. Even our fighting men overseas read about the escape in *Stars and Stripes,* the Armed Forces' newspaper.

A WW II Owosso soldier, fighting the Japanese in the Pacific, read the story in *Stars and Stripes* and was so enraged that he wrote a letter to the editor. He declared that Owosso people were patriotic Americans who would never condone the behavior of these two young women.

By all accounts, he was correct. Owosso citizens were very angry and ashamed of the women and their foolhardy acts.

So how did the two women fare in court? Mercifully, early in the proceedings, the federal district judge in Bay City, noting a lack of traitorous intent on the part of the women, ordered them to be tried on a reduced charge of conspiracy. Nonetheless, the jury found them both guilty as charged.

Despite pleas for leniency by the women's attorney, the judge's sentences were severe. One year and three months for Kitty Case, age twenty. One year and one day for Shirley Druce, age nineteen.

But according to Melinda Nethaway, that's not the end of the story. Nethaway, Druce's daughter-in-law, said that Druce was greatly ashamed of the incident and moved to California after serving out her prison term. Even though she was thousands of miles from Owosso, Nethaway said the incident haunted Druce for the rest of her life.

Nethaway, married to Druce's son Cary, said it was years before she learned about the POW escape, a closely guarded family secret. None of Druce's four children were aware of the incident until after she died.

What happened after Kitty Case was released from prison was never publicized. But the rumor was that Case had committed suicide shortly after her release from prison.

Author's Note. The incident involving Shirley Druce, Kitty Case, and the two German POWS became the genesis of my five, 400-page Cottonwood *novels that were published between 2004 and 2012. Each novel contains a unique storyline about POWs in America. Among my source materials, I recently rediscovered an article on the escape, written by Jim Dingwall,* Owosso Argus-Press *City Editor on June 28, 1962. (See Appendix F. POW Camp near Owosso Recalled.)*

"You stare at that fence for hours on end, try to think of everything and anything that can be done, and finally realize there are only three possibilities: go through it, fly over it, or dig under it. Conceiving of the tunnel, digging it, getting out, getting back, telling about our adventures, finding out what happened to the others … why, it covered a year or more and was our great recreation. It kept our spirits up even as Germany was being crushed and we worried about our parents and our families."

Lt. Wolfgang Clarus, German POW captured in North Africa.

7. POW Escapes

The risk of POW escapes greatly concerned America's military and political leaders. But POW escape attempts were extremely rare. Of the more than 435,000 POWs in America, only 2,827 escaped. Almost all were captured, returned on their own, or gave themselves up. Only twenty-two were never recaptured. Putting this in per-spective, the POW escape rate was far lower than that of the U.S. Federal Prison System at the time.

Incidentally, this low number of escapes existed despite the fact that their governments had informed POWs through the Red Cross of their rights under the Geneva Convention. These rights included the right to take every opportunity to escape.

Many factors influenced this low escape-attempt number. First, enemy officers and non-commissioned officers were imprisoned in the same camps as their enlisted POWs. The presence of the higher-ranked POWs solidified control over the enlisted men.

Presumably these officers did not believe that escapes served the POWs' best interests.

POWs had other reasons for wanting to remain in the camps:

1. There were numerous artistic, musical, athletic, and educational activities available to the POWs. These were provided by local organizations including:

   - War Prisoners Aid Committee
   - National Catholic Welfare Council
   - International Committee of the Red Cross

   The POWs chose to stay in camps to take advantage of these activities.

2. POWs were offered jobs in the community in which the camps were located. While the amount paid by farmers and factories for the services of POWs was approximately the same as that paid to American workers doing those jobs, the POWs received a fraction of what was charged. The minimum wage at the time was 50 cents per hour.

3. Finally, the size of America had something to do with the practicality of escaping. If a POW escaped, where would he go? And how would he get there?

Disharmony between the Nazis and anti-Nazis erupted in some camps and resulted in fourteen POWs sentenced to death for murdering their fellow POWs.

Most POWs escaped to break the monotony of camp or to seek the companionship of local young women they'd met at work.

The majority of the escaped prisoners returned on their own within twenty-four hours because they didn't want to miss the creature comforts of camp, including good food and a comfortable bed.

And where could they earn such good money? Or enjoy the extensive educational and recreational opportunities provided back at camp? In short, they had it pretty good.

However, there were a few determined POWs who earnestly attempted to escape. And, in a sense, you can't blame them. Being POWs, it was their duty. There was no provision in the Geneva Convention to prevent or condemn one for trying, the idea was that if you escaped or even attempted to escape, the enemy would be required to spend more resources tracking you down and guarding you. Obviously, some POWs took this duty very seriously, especially the Japanese. In all, fifty-six POWs were shot and killed while attempting to escape from camps on American soil.

The Great Escape

During a cold drizzle on Christmas Eve of 1944, a group of twenty-five German officers and enlisted men escaped through a tunnel from Camp Papago Park, located in Phoenix, Arizona. The camp was the repository of 1,700 of the most ardent Nazi POWs in America. The escape was led by Submarine Captain Jurgen Wattenberg, who believed fervently that escaping was his solemn duty.

The digging of the tunnel had been facilitated by camp guards, who willingly furnished digging tools to the POWs when they requested permission to build a volleyball court. Over the course of three months as the tunnel was being dug, the POWs stuffed dirt from the tunnel into pants' pockets with holes in the bottoms. To cover up their tunneling activities, they walked around camp to distribute the dirt evenly. Incredibly, the resultant tunnel was 178 feet long and three feet in diameter.

In the camp woodshop, the POWs constructed canoes in three sections to make it easier to transport them through the tunnel. The canoes were tested for watertightness in the camp showers and pronounced seaworthy.

From maps they had acquired, Wattenberg and his officers devised a plan calling for them to wade down the Cross-Cut Canal pulling their canoes behind them until they reached the Salt River. Once there, they would launch their canoes and float down to the Gila River and then on to the Colorado River that would take them into Mexico.

Under cover of a noisy Christmas party contrived by their fellow POWs, the officers and men made it through the tunnel with their canoes. When they arrived at their first destination, they were shocked to discover that the Salt River was nothing but a muddy bog created by the recent rains. But they failed to take into consideration that, like many of Arizona's rivers, the Salt was bone-dry most of the year.

Not to be discouraged, they carried their canoes another twenty miles to the Salt's confluence with the Gila River. There they discovered the Gila was nothing but a series of large puddles. The discouraged POWs sat on the riverbank with their heads in their hands and cried out of utter frustration.

Cold, wet, and hungry, Herbert Fuchs, one of the enlisted POWs, decided to throw in the towel. Flagging down an unsuspecting motorist, he requested to be taken to the sheriff's office, where he surrendered. The sheriff called the camp and told them that he had one of their prisoners who wanted to *come home*. Until the sheriff's call, camp officials were blissfully unaware of the escape.

Within days, all twenty-five POWs were returned to Camp Papago Park. Most required hospital treatment for exposure to the elements and exhaustion. This was not a glorious homecoming.

The Long Arm of the Law

Although the details are sketchy, the following case provides an important lesson. Never fool with the FBI.

A German POW, Ernst Meer, escaped from Camp Reynolds in Pennsylvania. He hopped a freight train that carried him to Kentucky, where he secured employment on a horse farm. After several weeks, he was tracked down by a diligent FBI agent named Johnson, who arrested him and returned him to Camp Reynolds.

Meer was not happy about his lost freedom. After a few weeks, he escaped a second time. This time his plan was to get as far away from Pennsylvania as he could. So, he hitchhiked to California, where he planned to enjoy life without constantly having to look over his shoulder.

Months later, Agent Johnson was in California investigating another case. Walking back to his hotel, Johnson just happened to spot Meer walking toward him on the opposite side of the street. He crossed the street and rearrested the POW.

Naturally Meer was impressed with Johnson's ability to track him down. So, he asked Johnson how he had done it.

Johnson simply replied, "We have our ways."

Mountain Law

Three German submariners, POWs at Camp Crossville, Tennessee, were assigned to a crew cutting timber in a remote area of the Cumberland Mountains. Left alone for a period, the trio decided to escape by fleeing into the dense forest.

They wandered aimlessly for several days, lost in the rugged mountain country. When they came upon a cabin in the woods, they attempted to get a drink of water from a pump. An irascible Granny appeared at the cabin door, aimed her squirrel rifle, and told them to *Git*!

Unschooled in the ways of mountain folks, the Germans ignored her. So, she took aim and fired, killing one of the Germans. When the sheriff informed her that she had killed a German POW, she broke into tears.

The puzzled sheriff asked, "Well, shucks, Granny. What did you think you wuz aiming at?"

She replied, "I thought they wuz Yankees!"

Minor Overnight Escapes

A German POW named Hoefer walked away from Camp Forrest, Tennessee, to the nearby town of Tullahoma. There he caught the morning train to Nashville. He met an American GI who was home on leave, and the two of them spent the night pub crawling.

The next morning, Hoefer was stopped for a routine check of his Selective Service card. Unable to produce one, the POW confessed and was promptly arrested. Soon thereafter, he was returned to Camp Forrest where, it is reported, he bragged about his short-lived adventure to his fellow POWs.

There were a number of other short and relatively harmless escapes from POW camps. The motivation for these overnight escapes was usually to break the monotony of camp or to seek the companionship of local women. These were more common than the escapes described above. And in nearly every case the POW involved had no intention of being without the creature comforts of POW camps for long. Escape attempts were relatively rare.

Escaped POWs Integrated into American Society

POW escapes were rare. As I mentioned earlier, of the nearly 435,000 POWs in America during the War, only 2,827 *escaped*. Most returned on their own for selfish reasons. They missed the comforts available in the POW camps.

Following are two cases of escaped German POWs recorded in Professor Arnold Krammer's book entitled *Nazi Prisoners of War in America,* published in 1979.

Georg Gaertner

German POW Georg Gaertner escaped from Camp Deming, New Mexico, by crawling under two gates and jumping onto a passing freight train. Gaertner, who spoke fluent English, was able to pass for an American and worked as a ski instructor in the winter and a tennis instructor in the summer.

Unexpectedly, in 1984, author Krammer received a call from a man who called himself Dennis Whiles. He told Krammer that he had spent a couple of years in a POW camp in New Mexico. Then he proceeded to regale Krammer with the usual stories of camp life: pranks on guards, plots, and the inevitable homemade wine, almost always hidden inside the pulpit of the camp chapel. After enjoying the stories for ten or fifteen minutes, Krammer told Whiles that he had to deliver a lecture and needed to end the conversation. Whiles' voice became very soft.

"But that was an important call for me. I realized that I was the last fugitive German POW. I escaped from Camp Deming in September 1945 and had been on the run for almost forty years."

Georg Gaertner publicly surrendered on public television in September 1985. His story appeared everywhere in the American press. No charges were filed against him, and he was allowed to remain in the United States and become a naturalized citizen. Gaetner later married, worked various jobs, and stayed in America until his death in 2013.

Krammer's later book entitled *Hitler's Last Soldier in America* was written with Gaetner's help.

Reinhold Papel

In Krammer's book, there is another story of an escaped German POW who successfully integrated into American society. Reinhold Papel, a former German infantry sergeant, escaped from Camp Washington near Peoria, Illinois, on September 9, 1945. He changed his name to *Phillip Brick* and assumed the identity of a Dutch refugee.

Remarkably Brick filed an income tax return and received a $72 rebate from the IRS. By working various jobs in Chicago over the following two years, he parlayed this rebate into enough money to open a tiny book shop. After a short period of success, he opened a larger bookstore, and his wealth grew considerably. He married, and the couple had their first child in 1952.

Ironically, as a bookstore owner, he experienced the secret pleasure of selling a book to a man he recognized as one of his former guards at the POW camp where he had been interned. I am not sure this *reunion* had anything to do with it, but a short time later, he was arrested by FBI agents in his bookstore.

Without spelling out the lengthy legal proceedings, in 1954, Papel was finally allowed to return to his native Hamburg, where he opened yet another bookstore.

Author's Note. During this period, I recall watching an Ed Sullivan television program where one of Ed's guests was an escaped German POW who had managed to escape and integrate into American society. During the POW's appearance, he basked in the warmth of celebrity status. Unfortunately, I don't recall the man's name, but I am sure he was one of the two POWs described in Krammer's book. In any case, this remarkable story has captivated my imagination for decades.

German and Japanese POW Worldwide Escapes

In Canada, there were about 600 escape attempts during the War, including at least two mass escapes through tunnels. Four

German POWs were killed attempting to escape from Canadian prison camps, while three others were wounded.

Most escapees tried to reach the United States when it was still neutral, though Karl Heinz-Grund and Horst Liebeck made it as far as Medicine Hat, Alberta, before being apprehended by the Royal Canadian Mounted Police. The two men had planned to travel to Vancouver, British Columbia, and leave Canada courtesy of the Japanese merchant marine.

October 7, 1940. December 20, 1940. January 21, 1941. Great Britain to Germany.

On his first solo attempt to escape from Camp Grizedale Hall, Franz von Werra was recaptured on October 12. His second attempt involved four others, who were quickly caught. He was recaptured while trying to steal an airplane. He was then shipped from Great Britain to Canada, where, on his third attempt, he jumped out of the window of a moving train. Seven others were recaptured. Von Werra made his way first to the United States, still neutral at that time, then to Mexico before he could be extradited back to Canada and eventually to Nazi Germany. He is the only German World War II POW to escape and return to Germany.

April 18, 1941. Ontario, Canada.

Twenty-eight Germans escaped from a POW camp in Angler, Ontario, through a 150-foot long tunnel. Originally, over eighty had planned to escape, but Canadian guards discovered the breakout in progress. Two prisoners were killed and the others recaptured.

November 23, 1941, December 1941 and February 18, 1942. Ontario to Niagara Falls.

A Luftwaffe Oberleutnant and Ace, Ulrich Steinhilper, escaped from Bowmanville Camp, Ontario, and managed to arrive at Niagara Falls in two days. Unknowingly, Steinhilper had spent thirty minutes in the neutral United States, clinging beneath a train car, parked in a Buffalo, New York railyard. In less than three weeks, he escaped again and made it as far as Montreal, Quebec.

Within four months, Steinhilper attempted yet a third escape. On February 18, 1942, Steinhilper and a friend, disguised as painters, used a ladder to escape over two barbed wire fences. The pair traveled as far as Watertown, New York, before being arrested by police. Steinhilper was then sent to Gravenhurst, Ontario, where he attempted two further escapes.

November 24, 1941. United Kingdom.
At RAF Carlisle, United Kingdom, Luftwaffe pilots, Heinz Schnabel and Harry Wappler, stole a Miles Magister trainer aircraft and flew to several other RAF airfields before being recaptured.

April 17, 1942 and October 1943. Ontario, Canada to Texas.
Dornier Do-17 bomber pilot, Oberleutnant Peter Krug, made it as far as San Antonio, Texas from the Bowmanville, Ontario POW camp. The young Luftwaffe pilot was aided in his flight by Axis sympathizers in the United States, whose addresses may have been procured from outside sources. His second escape was from Gravenhurst, Ontario. He was caught after twenty-four hours, according to the October 5, 1943 edition of the *North Bay Nugget* newspaper.

November 1, 1942. New Mexico.
Four German POWs, including Bruno Dathe, Willy Michel, Hermann Runne, and Johannes Grantz, escaped from Fort Stanton, New Mexico and were captured two days later, after a brief skirmish with a posse of ranchers and cattlemen. One escapee was wounded.

January 1943. Camp 354, Kenya.
Italian POW Felice Benuzzi convinced two of his fellow inmates, Dr. Giovanni Balletto and Enzo Barsotti, to try an unusual escape

route by climbing nearby Mount Kenya. After eighteen days, they gave up and sneaked back into camp. After the war, Benuzzi wrote of his experience in *No Picnic on Mount Kenya.*

January 6, March 13, and April 18, 1943. Canada.
Karl Rabe of submarine U-35 tried, on four separate occasions, to escape from Lethbridge, Alberta, Canada. In one attempt, he used a twenty-four-by-ten-foot handmade, hot air balloon.

Previously he had escaped from a Toronto hospital, subsequently stealing a small row boat with the intention of crossing Lake Ontario to the American shore. But he beached the craft too soon, mistakenly thinking he was already on the American side. He was immediately recaptured by Canadian soldiers.

August 26, 1943. Canada.
Nineteen German POWs escaped through a large drainage pipe from Kingston, Ontario, Canada. All were soon recaptured.

September 26, 1943. Canada.
In Operation Kiebitz, at Bowmanville POW camp in Canada, Admiral Karl Dönitz sent the submarine U-536 to pick up four U-boat commanders, including noted ace Otto Kretschmar, who were to break out at a specified time. The Canadians were aware of the attempt but let it proceed, hoping to lure in the U-boat. However, the plan was aborted when part of their escape tunnel collapsed, revealing its exit to the guards.

Instead, another U-boat commander, Wolfgang Heyda, escaped over a barbed-wire fence and made his way some 870 miles to the rendezvous point. There he was captured, while the authorities waited for the U-boat to surface. Despite being spotted by three destroyers, it got away.

April 29, 1944. India to Tibet.
Heinrich Harrer, Peter Aufschnaiter, Hans Kopp and four others escaped from a British POW camp in Dehradun, the capital of Uttarakhand in India. Harrer and Aufschnaiter reached Lhasa and stayed with the Dalai Lama for seven years, finally escaping from Tibet ahead of the People's Liberation Army in 1950.

Rolf Margene and Hens von Have went east, passing through Burma and across the front line to reach Japanese troops. They reached Japan after four months on the run, but they returned to Germany two years after the end of the War.

August 5, 1944. Australia.
In the Cowra breakout in Australia, 359 Japanese POWs escaped in one of the largest breakouts of the war. All who were not killed or did not commit suicide were caught.

August 8, 1944. Ontario, Canada.
Luftwaffe Lieutenant Walter Manhard successfully escaped by a tunnel from a POW camp in Gravenhurst, Ontario. He was presumed drowned during the escape attempt. But, in 1952, he gave himself up to New York State authorities. By then, he was married to a United States naval officer.

August 30, 1944. Alberta, Canada.
Deutsches Afrikakorps (DAK) soldier Max Weidauer escaped from Medicine Hat, Alberta, after he came under suspicion by Nazi elements controlling the camp and the subsequent murder of fellow DAK prisoner, August Plaszek.

After explaining the circumstances of his escape and the fact that he feared for his life, Weidauer was hidden by a local farmer. He was soon once again behind barbed wire, though in a different camp.

December 24, 1944. United States.
Papago Park, United States. Twenty-five prisoners escaped through a tunnel, but all were recaptured. On January 28, 1945, U-boat commander Jürgen Wattenberg was the last to be recaptured.

March 10, 1945. United Kingdom.
Island Farm, United Kingdom. Seventy, possibly more, escaped, but all were recaptured.

"If there was an additional lesson to be learned from the issue of prisoner escapes, it was that the greatest danger did not lie with the few men who escaped but with the thousands of hardened Nazis who remained behind."

From *Nazi Prisoners of War in America* by Arnold Krammer.

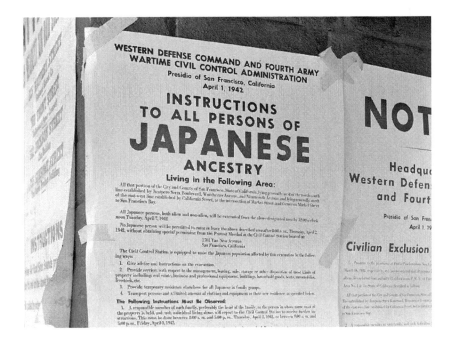

The 1942 Internment instructions for Japanese Americans living in the United States. *Photo from the National Archives. Identifier: 520992.*

8. American Citizens in American Internment Camps

Japanese-American Internment

After the attack on Pearl Harbor by Japanese aircraft on December 7, 1941, the U.S. War Department suspected that Japanese Americans might act as saboteurs or espionage agents despite a lack of hard evidence to support this view. Some political leaders recommended rounding up Japanese Americans, particularly those living along the West Coast, and placing them in detention camps inland.

A power struggle erupted between the U.S. Department of Justice, which opposed moving innocent civilians, and the War Department, which favored detention.

John J. McCloy, the Assistant Secretary of War, remarked that if it was a choice between national security and the guarantee of civil liberties expressed in the Constitution, he considered the Constitution *just a scrap of paper*. In the immediate aftermath of the Pearl Harbor attack, 1200 Japanese community leaders were arrested and the assets of their accounts in the U.S. branches of Japanese banks were frozen.

At the time of the Pearl Harbor attack, approximately 125,000 Japanese Americans lived on the mainland in the United States. Another 200,000 had immigrated to Hawaii, then a U.S. territory.

Some first-generation Japanese Americans, known as *Issei*, had emigrated from Japan and were not eligible for U.S. citizenship.

About 80,000 of them, second-generation individuals born in the United States (*Nisei*), were U.S. citizens. Many Issei retained their Japanese character and culture. Nisei generally acted and thought of themselves as thoroughly American.

In early February 1942, the War Department created twelve restricted zones along the Pacific coast and established nighttime curfews for Japanese Americans. Individuals who broke the curfew were subject to immediate arrest. The nation's political leaders still debated the question of relocation, and the issue was soon decided.

On February 19, 1942, President Franklin D. Roosevelt signed Executive Order 9066, which gave the U.S. military authority to exclude any persons from designated areas. Although the word *Japanese* did not appear in the executive order, it was clear that only Japanese Americans were targeted, though some other immigrants, including Germans and Italians would also face detention during the War.

On March 18, 1942, the federal War Relocation Authority (WRA) was established. Its mission was to "take all people of Japanese descent into custody, surround them with troops, prevent them from buying land, and return them to their former homes at the close of the War."

The Japanese Americans were forced to sell their property, including businesses, within two weeks. Some non-Japanese Americans seized the opportunity of this situation, offering unreasonably low sums to buy possessions from those being forced to move.

On April 1, 1942, after being forcibly removed from their homes, Japanese Americans were first taken to temporary assembly centers. From there they were transported inland to internment camps. Between 1942 and 1945, ten camps were opened in California, Arizona, Wyoming, Colorado, Utah, and Arkansas.

Conditions at the camps were sparse. The internees lived in uninsulated barracks furnished with only cots and coal-burning stoves. Residents used common bathroom and laundry facilities, but hot water was usually limited.

There were a few isolated incidents of internees being shot and killed, as well as numerous examples of preventable suffering.

Residents lived in family groups, and the internees set up schools, churches, farms, and newspapers. Children played sports and engaged in various activities. However, the internment took its toll on Japanese Americans, who spent as long as three years living in an atmosphere of tension, suspicion, and despair.

On December 17, 1944, President Franklin D. Roosevelt signed a proclamation allowing internees to return to their homes, but most remained in the camps for another year because of the threatening anti-Japanese sentiment. About 55,000 returned to life outside the barbed wire.

Those who returned to the West Coast found their property vandalized, farms gone to seed, and businesses bankrupt.

Japanese Americans lost nearly half a billion dollars in assets. Many never recovered their losses and were forced to live in poverty. When the War ended, about 8,000 *renunciants,* Japanese Americans who had renounced their American citizenship while in the camps, were sent back to Japan.

In 1976, President Gerald R. Ford officially repealed Executive Order 9066. He used that opportunity to express regret for that policy:

"February 19th is the anniversary of a sad day in American history. It was on that day in 1942 that Executive Order 9066 was issued resulting in the uprooting of loyal Americans. We now know what we should have known then, not only was that evacuation wrong, but Japanese Americans were and are loyal Americans. I call upon the American people to affirm with me this American Promise, that we have learned from the tragedy of that long-ago experience forever to treasure liberty and justice for each individual American, and to resolve that this kind of action shall never again be repeated."

On August 10, 1988, President Reagan signed the Civil Liberties Act of 1988, which provided an apology and redress to internees still living. However, nearly half of the internees had died in the intervening forty-four years. In 1990, the government issued a formal apology together with a check for $20,000 to each surviving internee. This payment covered only about ten percent of their sustained losses.

The Japanese-American 442nd Regimental Combat Team

After the December 7, 1941 attack on the U.S. naval base at Pearl Harbor, Hawaii, the loyalty of all those of Japanese descent living in America, regardless of their citizenship status, was called into question. In Hawaii, where ethnic Japanese accounted for more than one-third of the island's population, first generation

Japanese (Issei) and the second generation (Nisei) faced similar suspicions. Although few Japanese in Hawaii were relocated, their freedoms were severely curtailed. Many military advisors expressed concerns over the loyalty of Japanese residents serving in the Armed Forces, and efforts were soon underway to remove those who had served prior to Pearl Harbor.

Members of the Hawaii National Guard were temporarily disarmed, and local ROTC students and cadets were dismissed from service. Determined to prove their loyalty to the United States and come to the defense of their fellow Hawaiians, these former servicemen formed a civilian aide group, the Varsity Victory Volunteers (VVV), which provided the physical labor needed for the massive construction of U.S. military bases in the Pacific.

Impressed with the VVV's determination and swayed by vocal protests over treatment of the Nisei soldiers, the War Department reversed course, announcing the formation of an all-Nisei combat unit, the 100th Infantry Battalion. After nearly a year of training on the U.S. mainland, the 100th was deployed to North Africa in September 1943, where it participated in the attacks on Monte Cassino, the breakout from Anzio, and the final Allied offensive push from Rome to the Arno River. In August of that year, the 100th was reorganized and became a part of the 442nd Regimental Combat Team (RCT), another Japanese-American unit, under which it served for the duration of the War.

While the 442nd RCT included additional soldiers from Hawaii, it was primarily composed of volunteers from Japanese internment camps and Japanese Americans who had served in the U.S. Army prior to the War. In June 1944, they, too, were deployed to Europe. There they fought in eight major campaigns in France, Italy, and Germany. In October of that year, they played a key role in the bloody rescue of the Lost Battalion, an Allied unit that had been trapped and surrounded by Axis forces in the Vosges Forest in France. In April 1945, many men of the 442nd had family members living in U.S. internment camps. The 442nd was among the first Allied troops to participate in the liberation of the Nazi concentration camp at Dachau, a sobering experience that would haunt many of them for decades. Eventually, more than 13,000 soldiers served in the regiment, with more than 700 members killed or missing in action.

The 442nd became the most decorated unit of its size in U.S. military history. In less than two years of combat, the unit earned more than 18,000 awards, including 9,486 Purple Hearts, 4,000 Bronze Stars, and 21 Medals of Honor. Upon return to the United States, they were praised by President Harry Truman for their brave stand both at home and abroad. And they were the subject of the 1951 film, *Go for Broke*. The film's title was derived from the unit's official slogan. Many members of the 442nd went on to distinguished careers in science, academia, and government, including the nine-term U.S. Senator Daniel Inouye from Hawaii, who lost an arm due to World War II combat injuries.

German-American Internment

Internment of Japanese Americans during World War II is widely known and well documented. However, less is known about the thousands of ethnic Germans who were also interned.

By 1940, the ethnic Germans made up a large percentage of the non-American population of the United States. Approximately 1.2 million German nationals and 11 million U.S. citizens had at least one German-born parent. Then, the 1940 census introduced a new requirement. Now it mandated that all respondents include their ethnicity. Also, in 1940, a new law was passed requiring all aliens over the age of fourteen to register.

Following the Japanese attack on Pearl Harbor in 1941 but before America declared war on Germany, President Franklin Roosevelt announced that Germans, Italians, and Japanese were considered enemy aliens.

Anyone considered an ethnic German came under suspicion. Cases were considered on an individual basis. In theory, people were only to be detained if there was some evidence to suggest they posed a threat.

As a result, 11,000 people were taken to Department of Justice (DOJ) camps. The majority of these were German nationals, but the number also included U.S. citizens of German descent. The number of those who spent the War in such camps was, in fact, much higher than the 11,000 detainees. Why? Only enemy aliens could be interned by law.

But their families could come along voluntarily. Although living in the DOJ Camp wasn't ideal, many chose this option rather than to be separated. In addition, families could be left without income if the income earner was detained in camp.

The government set up four camps. The main ones were located in Hot Springs, California, and at Fort Oglethorpe, Georgia. These camps provided many facilities that families required, including doctors and schools that offered German lessons. Family life was able to continue. In fact, 153 children were born in the camp. This resulted in American spouses and their children spending the war years in these DOJ camps.

If both parents were ethnic Germans, children were placed in orphanages while their parents were in detention. Even those not detained were restricted. They were banned from certain areas and subjected to curfew laws.

The American camps also held a large number of Germans who had been living in Latin America. It is estimated that over 4,000 people were expelled and sent to America to be interned. Some of these were Nazi party members assigned to the overseas branch of the party. Eight of these individuals were suspected of spying for Germany.

Not every Latin American country deported their German population. Several, including Brazil, Mexico, and Venezuela, established their own camps.

After Germany surrendered, many of the internees were released and sent to Germany. Others remained in the camps. It was not until 1948 that the last enemy alien was released. None of these internees was ever found guilty of a crime or proved to be a threat to national security.

Those who were released were obliged to sign a secrecy agreement regarding the time spent in camp. They were under threat of being returned to Germany if they breached the terms of the agreement.

In 2005, the German-American Internee Coalition was formed to campaign on behalf of those detained. They wanted recognition of this infringement of their rights, as well as reparation.

There was some support within the government, so a review commission was established in 2005. This led to the drafting of a law entitled the Wartime Study Act in 2007. Unfortunately, it never became law, and no further action was taken.

Italian-American Internment

During the War, there were a number of Italian nationals interned, similar to the internment of German Americans. After Italy and America were at war, the Italian Americans were classified as enemy aliens and some were detained by the Department of Justice under the Alien and Sedition Act. But in practice, the U.S. government applied detention only to Italian nationals, not to U.S. citizens or long-term U.S. residents. By 1940, there were millions of U.S. citizens who had been born in Italy.

By 1942, there were 695,000 Italian immigrants in the United States. Some 1,881 were taken into custody and detained under wartime restrictions. Most often, the United States Department of Justice detained diplomats, businessmen, and Italian nationals who were students in the United States, especially excluding them from sensitive coastal areas. In addition, merchant seamen trapped in U.S. ports by the outbreak of the War were detained. Italian labor leaders lobbied for their recognition as loyal Italian Americans who had initiated naturalization before the war broke out. They objected to blanket classification of all Italian nationals as subversives.

The members of the ethnic Italian community in America presented an unusual problem. Defined in terms of national origin, it was the largest ethnic community in the United States, having been supplied by a steady flow of Italian immigrants between 1880 and 1930. By 1940, in the United States there were millions of native-born Italians who had become American citizens. There were also a great many Italian enemy aliens, more than 600,000, who had immigrated during the previous decades and had not become naturalized American citizens of the United States.

Many Italian families had been in this country for decades but were technically classified as enemy aliens. So, the problem of assessing the circumstances of each case was a long and difficult process. And because we were at war with Italy, decisions had to be made on the basis of commonsense and what was in the best interest of America.

Even today, some Italian Americans resent that their ancestors were classified as enemy aliens by the U.S. government. On balance, our government took great care to make the right decisions in these cases.

A young evacuee of Japanese ancestry from San Francisco waits with the family baggage before leaving by bus for an assembly center in the spring of 1942. *Photo from the National Archives. Identifier: 539959*

On July 4, 1942, American POWs celebrated the 4th of July in a Japanese prison camp on Mindanao, Philippine Islands. While it was against Japanese regulations and discovery would have meant death, the men celebrated anyway. *Photo from the National Archives. Identifier: 531352.*

9. American Prisoners in Axis POW Camps

On December 7, 1941, 353 aircraft from the Empire of Japan attacked the American naval base at Pearl Harbor, Hawaii, and inflicted mass destruction of American life and property. In response, on December 8th, the U.S. declared war on Japan. Three days later, Italian dictator Benito Mussolini declared war on America. From the balcony over the Piazza Venezia in Rome, he pledged "the powers of the pact of steel" were determined to win.

Then, Adolf Hitler made his declaration at the Reichstag in Berlin. Hitler stated that he had tried to avoid direct conflict with the United States, but under the Tripartite Pact signed on September 27, 1940, Germany was obliged to join with Italy to defend its ally Japan. Hitler stated, "After victory has been achieved, Germany, Italy, and Japan will continue in closest cooperation with a view to establish a new and just order."

Americans in German POW Camps

Over 16 million Americans served in World War II. Of these, over 120,000 spent part of the War behind barbed wire in Axis POW camps. In Europe, there were 93,941 American POWs in German camps. These *Kriegies,* short for Kriegsgefangener (German for POWs), counted the days until liberation and created dream worlds for themselves inside the camps.

During the War, Germany imprisoned more Americans than its allies, Italy and Japan. As a signatory of the Geneva Convention and fearful of reprisals against the 390,000 German POWs held in POW camps in America, Germany generally adhered to the measures outlined for the humane treatment of POWs until the collapse of Hitler's government in 1944.

However, American POWs interned by Germany's ally Japan were not protected by such constraints. As prisoners of the Germans during World War II, life was difficult, often boring, and above all, uncertain. The 92,820 American POWs in German camps lived to tell of their experiences.

Capture

Whether they surrendered alone or with others, the first weeks of captivity were always anxious ones for a new POW. In 1943, most American POWs were airmen, who descended at the average rate of 400 men per month. In June 1944, the Germans held as many U.S. airmen as ground force troops. This situation reversed itself after the conclusion and heavy losses at the Battle of the Bulge in December 1944. There, nearly 23,000 Americans, mainly infantrymen, were captured by the Germans.

In letters sent thousands of miles across the globe, families on the home front detailed their everyday lives in a struggle to maintain contact with their loved ones. Some letters were returned unopened, marked *Missing*. In many cases, it was months before word was received confirming captivity or worse.

The Letter

The Adjutant General's office was responsible for sending the official word on a serviceman's status to his next of kin. However, the responsibility for reporting to various nations about the circumstances involving a serviceman's captivity fell to the International Red Cross, based in Geneva, Switzerland. The Red Cross's efforts were directed by the Central Information Agency on POWs, which maintained a massive card index that tracked some forty-five million prisoners from all countries.

Communications and delivery of over 120 million messages proved a bureaucratic nightmare. But this played a significant factor in shaping the morale and maintaining sanity on the home front and on the battlefield.

Camp Life

The experience of captivity was a *life within a life* for many Americans. With the primary objectives of combat no longer applying to them, boredom, futility, and helplessness became enemies to be combated as tenaciously as the Nazis. After interrogation, most prisoners were assigned to a permanent camp based on their rank and then transported to widely varying environments, mainly based on location of the fighting and the state of the War.

Americans were typically housed adjacent to, but separate from, the British and the other Allied prisoners. These accommodations ranged from wooden barracks to concrete cells with a capacity of eight to forty men. Fortunately, the meager daily ration of food provided was supplemented with provisions from the Red Cross. Food was often communally cooked on stoves in the barracks.

Attempts to prevent becoming *wire happy*, included setting up classrooms and offering courses in what became known as *Barbed Wire Universities*. Some camps contained libraries of up to 15,000 volumes, everything but spy-and-escape stories. The prisoners maintained a list of all the books they read during their confinement.

Sporting events were held, using equipment supplied by the YMCA. Boxing matches, track meets, football and baseball games were very popular.

Camp theaters produced shows, especially comedies, and even printed tickets and playbills listing the casts.

In addition to these recreational and education occupations, trying to escape occupied time and provided a sense of duty fulfilled. Staying connected and alive had become a full-time endeavor.

Red Cross in POW Life

One of the primary tasks of the Red Cross was to monitor the health and well-being of POWs. Among other things, it was responsible for overseeing distribution of food, medicine, and mail. The American Red Cross played a vital role in POW life during WWII, particularly in Europe, where they distributed more than twenty-seven million parcels to U.S. and Allied prisoners of war.

These packages were assembled by the mass effort of more than 13,000 volunteers in its distribution centers around the United States. POWs were intended to receive one Red Cross parcel per week. The packages contained nonperishable foods like biscuits, raisins, coffee, powdered milk, and canned beef and fish, along with amenities like cigarettes and soap. The boxes were received by American POW representatives in the camps and collected for fair and orderly disbursement. In addition, special Christmas parcels were sent with holiday treats.

As War conditions worsened for the Germans and bombing of German supply lines increased, the receipt of aid packages dwindled. POWs captured late in the War reported very little contact with the Red Cross. These care packages and the supplemental nourishment that they provided were a crucial part of POW survival, helping to sustain both body and soul during captivity.

Liberation

In 1944, as the War began to shift in favor of the Allies, conditions in POW camps worsened. Overcrowding and disease increased, as did the dangers of Allied bombing. Rumors swirled among prisoners about liberation, but also about doubts that the Germans would allow them to be liberated. Life became even more uncertain for the thousands of POWs held widely across Europe as Germany began to shift men, including POWs, into the inner core of their territory.

In harsh winter weather between January and April of 1945, 80,000 Allied POWs were marched westward ahead of the Soviet Army. Referred to as the *Long March*, *Long Trek*, or *Black March*, it is believed that some 3,500 American and Commonwealth POWs died during these marches. By May 20, 1945, all surviving

American POWs were back in American hands. It would take many more months before Recovered Allied Military Personnel (RAMPS) would be home, ending one chapter in their lives to begin another.

War Crimes: Berga and Malmedy

Experiences lived during the global conflict of WWII are as different as every man who served. Conditions for POWs under the Germans varied greatly, and not all American POWs were afforded the protection of the Geneva Convention.

At Stalag IXB in January 1945, 350 American POWs were selected to be sent to Berga slave labor camp because they were Jewish. There they endured inhumane treatment as laborers in the underground tunnels along with prisoners from the nearby Buchenwald concentration camp. All suffered from starvation and beatings. Eighty-six of these men died before being liberated.

On December 17, 1944, outside of Malmedy, Belgium, eighty-four American POWs were murdered by their German captors, part of the 1st SS Panzer Division. The War crime now known as the Malmedy Massacre was part of a series of such killings in which 132 American POWs and over 100 Belgian civilians perished.

Repatriation

Under the rules of the Geneva Convention, gravely ill prisoners of war had the right to be evaluated by a physician from the captor's country, along with the International Red Cross, to deem if their wounds were severe enough to call for repatriation in a prisoner exchange with Germany.

After the Camps' Invisible Walls

Dreaming of the life that would come after liberation sustained many during captivity. However, following liberation, it was not easy to accept reality. Former POW Lieutenant John Poppinger stated in a poem:

"It takes a little while to get reacquainted with Miss Freedom when you haven't seen her for a long time."

While some POWs began to meet after the War to talk about their shared experiences, others repressed memories of their time in captivity and tried to put the horrific barbed wire world behind them. Like many other combat stories, POW memoirs emerged only after the distance in time had been bridged.

Some returned with narratives composed in the camps, or shortly thereafter, and shaped them into life stories. In other cases, the POW stories remained unread until their authors' deaths, only discovered by family members after the opportunity for questions was gone. Through these tales and through the discoveries of the next generation, we are able to explore the sufferings and successes of the *Kriegies*.

Monopoly Game

In 2007, long after the War ended, according to the terms of the Official Secrets Act of 1939, the British government declassified information relating to how the popular Monopoly game played an important role in winning World War II.

Beginning in 1941, a great number of the British airmen found themselves imprisoned in POW camps behind German lines and in need of maps to assist them in escaping. Paper maps were noisy when crinkled, often wore out before they could be used, and turned to mush when wet. For hundreds of years, even before World War II, silk was the material of choice for military maps. Silk didn't tear or dissolve in water as easily as paper and was light enough to stuff in a boot or cigarette package.

MI9, the British secret service, contacted John Waddington Ltd., a British company that had perfected the technology for printing on silk. Coincidentally. this firm was also the British licensee for the Parker Brothers game of Monopoly.

The German army allowed humanitarian groups to distribute care packages to imprisoned soldiers. The game of Monopoly was too innocent looking to raise any suspicion. But it was the ideal size for a top-secret escape kit that could be used to assist British POWs to escape from German POW camps.

Maps were folded and inserted in a Monopoly playing piece. Another small piece held a magnetic compass. Small metal tools were included. High-denomination German, Italian, or French currency was hidden in stacks of Monopoly play money. British and American crews were told to look for special edition Monopoly sets. These would be marked with a red dot, which looked like a printing error, in the Free Parking square.

A small, sworn-to-secrecy division of Waddington printed silk and rayon maps that depicted routes to locations of safe houses and other places where escaped prisoners could find refuge. These maps covered the regions where POW camps were located. Codes printed on the box covers assured that each set reached its designated camp.

Before leaving for missions over Germany, the British airmen were instructed that, when captured, they should look for escape maps and kits in Monopoly as well as other games delivered by charity groups. Waddington printed six different maps that corresponded with regions surrounding six different German POW camps. The Monopoly kit bound for a camp in Italy, for example, included a map of Italy and Italian currency (lira).

To ensure each set reached its destination, the secret service devised a special code. Each map was pinpointed to a camp location. To tag each board game innocuously, a period was added after different locations on the board.

A period after Mayfair, for example, meant the game was intended for Norway, Sweden, and Germany. And a period after Marylebone Station meant the game was destined for Italy. Being a British version of the game, London streets replaced the Atlantic City streets used in the original American version. During the War, hundreds of thousands of silk maps were used to help prisoners escape.

Americans in Italian POW Camps

German and Italian forces in North Africa surrendered on May 13, 1943. On July 9, 1943, the Allied Forces invaded Sicily. Shortly thereafter, on July 25, 1943, Benito Mussolini, the Italian dictator, resigned from his positions as head of the Italian armed forces and the Italian government.

King Victor Emmanuel assumed control of the army and appointed Marshall Pietro Badoglio as the new prime minister. Shortly thereafter, he assumed control of Italy itself. During the three days following the installation of the new government, the Italian people celebrated wildly. Italy was the first member of the Tripartite Pact to surrender to the Allies.

On September 8, 1943, at time of the Italian Armistice, there were some 80,000 Allied POWs in Italian camps. Among these POWs were 1,310 Americans, most of whom were soldiers who been captured in North Africa or airmen shot down over Italy.

The American POWs were confined at Camp 59, at Servigliano. This camp held about 3,000 prisoners, mostly Allied enlisted personnel. Although the camp was well-guarded and thorough searches were conducted frequently, numerous tunneling projects were continually in progress. While there were a number of escapes, most prisoners were recaptured.

When the Allied POWs learned of the Armistice, they were in a quandary as to what action to take. Under orders received earlier in the summer, most remained in their camps under the mistaken impression that Allied forces would soon liberate them. Italian camp authorities were also confused. Without clear orders, many simply opened the gates and allowed the Allied POWs to leave the camps.

During the first days after the Armistice, about 60,000 Allied POWs remained in their camps and quickly became prisoners of the Germans. Another 30,000 left their camps. Some 16,000 were recaptured by the Germans. Four thousand of them found safety in Switzerland. The remaining 10,000 found safety in hiding with the help of Italians, and many found their way back to Allied lines. Without this help, many of the escapees would have been recaptured and most likely ended up in German POW camps for the duration of the War.

At the signing of the Armistice, the Camp 59 Commandant, apparently a hard-core Italian Fascist, placed his guards around the walls of the camp, ostensibly to protect the prisoners from the Germans but in reality, to detain them until the arrival of the

Germans. On September 14th, it was rumored in the camp that the Germans were close by, and at 10:00 p.m. the Senior British Officer (SBO) gave the order to evacuate the camp. As the prisoners approached the gate, the guards opened fire, and the SBO went to the Commandant and asked, or perhaps threatened, that the guards be ordered to cease fire. The order was given over the loudspeaker, and the gates were opened.

When the gates were opened, the prisoners fled to get as far away as possible before the Germans arrived in the area. All of the prisoners made it to the Allied lines, some in 1943 and others in 1944. During the process, some were recaptured but escaped again, most likely with help from Italians. Without this aid, many of the escapees would have been recaptured and held in a German POW camp until the War ended.

Americans in Japanese POW Camps

Of the three Axis nations, Japan was, by far, the worst in terms of the treatment of its prisoners of war. The following statistics alone tell the story:

Percentage of American POWs that Died

American POWs held by Japanese – 33.0%
American POWs held by Germans – 1.19%

The Empire of Japan had signed but never ratified the 1929 Geneva Convention of the Prisoners of War. The Japanese did not treat POWs in accordance with any international agreements, including the Hague Convention, because the Japanese viewed surrender as dishonorable.

The Japanese believed it was a soldier's duty to fight to the death. That is why we captured 379,000 German POWs and only 5,000 Japanese POWs. The only way we *captured* a Japanese soldier was to find him wounded and unconscious on the battlefield. That is also why, when we transported Japanese POWs back to Japan after the War, fifty percent of them took their own lives by jumping overboard from our ships and drowning.

In Japanese camps, POWs from China, the United States, Australia, Britain, Canada, the Netherlands, New Zealand, and the Philippines were subject to murder, brutal beatings, forced labor, medical experimentation, starvation rations, poor medical treatment, and cannibalism.

After March 20, 1943, the Japanese Imperial Navy was ordered to execute all prisoners taken at sea.

Japanese in Allied POW Camps

It is important to point out that, despite the treatment of Allied POWs in Japanese POW camps, Japanese POWs held in Allied POW camps were treated in accordance with the rules spelled out in the Geneva Convention. By 1943, the Allied governments were well aware that personnel who had been captured by the Japanese military were being held in harsh conditions. In an attempt to win better treatment for their POWs, the Allies made extensive efforts to notify the Japanese government of the good conditions in Allied POW camps.

This was not successful, however, because the Japanese government refused to recognize the existence of captured Japanese military personnel, since they had been ordered not to surrender but to fight to the death. Nevertheless, Japanese

POWs in Allied camps continued to be treated in accordance with the Geneva Convention until the end of the War.

Most Japanese captured by Allied forces after September 1942 were turned over to Australia or New Zealand for internment. The United States provided these countries with aid through the Lend Lease program to cover the costs of maintaining the prisoners and for repatriating the men to Japan at the end of the War.

The 5,000 Japanese prisoners captured in the central Pacific or those who were believed to have particular intelligence value were held in camps in the United States. Those prisoners who chose to and were approved by the camp authorities were allowed to leave the camps to work on farms. According to the Geneva Convention, they were paid for their work, usually at somewhat less than an American might have made.

Unfortunately, sometimes Allied POW camps and transport ships were accidental targets of Allied attacks. A high number of deaths occurred when Japanese *hell ships*, unmarked transport ships in which POWs were transported in harsh conditions, were attacked by U.S. Navy submarines. It was estimated that one in three Allied prisoners in Japanese vessels was killed on the water by Allied fire.

In Japanese camps, atrocities inflicted on Allied POWs were painted by artists, including Jack Bridger Chalker, Philip Meninsky, Ashley George Old, and Ronald Searle. Human hair was often used for brushes, plant juices and blood for paint, and toilet paper as the canvas. Some of their works were used as evidence in trials of Japanese war criminals.

Female prisoners, detained at Changi POW camp in Singapore, bravely recorded their defiance in seemingly harmless prison quilt embroidery.

Japanese Internment and Concentration Camps

The list of Japanese camps is extraordinarily long. It includes a total of 212 military prisoner of war and civilian internment and concentration camps, constructed in the following locations:

- The Philippines
- Malaya and Singapore
- Formosa (Taiwan)
- North Borneo
- Sarawak
- China
- Manchuria
- Dutch East Indies
- Thailand and Burma
- New Guinea
- Portuguese Timor
- Hong Kong
- Japan

The number and location of these camps reflects the size of the conquered areas that Japan amassed during the decade between the mid-thirties and mid-forties.

The number of Allied prisoners, both military and civilian, is impossible to ascertain. But one can assume that the number was several thousands.

"[...] during one train stop, I watched as another guard with a spirit of empathy, ran out into an apple orchard and picked apples. He carried his jacket like a bag and filled it with apples. The kind German came to our open train window and handed us each an apple. The juicy apple tasted so delicious. I so appreciated that apple and his unusual compassion."

From *Prisoner of War Number 21860: The World War II Memoirs of Oliver Omanson* by Oliver Omanson

"The most vital lesson to be learned from the Holocaust era is that Auschwitz was possible because the enemy succeeded in dividing, in separating, in splitting human society, nation against nation, Christian against Jew, young against old. And not enough people cared."

Elie Wiesel, Romanian-born American writer, professor, political activist, Nobel laureate, and Holocaust survivor.

10. Other POWs in Axis Camps

Nazi Concentration and Extermination Camps

Holocaust is a Hebrew and Yiddish word meaning *sacrifice by fire*. The Holocaust was a systematic, state-sponsored campaign of murder and persecution that began in Germany in 1933 with racially discriminatory laws that expanded to the mass murder of all European Jews.

Adolph Hitler, cunning and tyrannical leader of the Nazi party, espoused the idea that Germans were a superior race. Therefore, any race, religion, or political philosophy not genetically a part of or in agreement with the viewpoint of the superior German race was deemed an enemy of the German state. The hatred of such internal and external enemies fed Germany's lust for blood and conquest.

Inferior groups included not only millions of Jews but tens of thousands of Roma or Gypsies and 200,000 mentally or physically handicapped people. More than three million Soviet prisoners of war, supposedly protected by the Geneva Convention, were murdered or died of starvation, disease, or maltreatment. The Nazis killed tens of thousands of non-Jewish Polish intellectual and religious leaders. Other *inferiors* persecuted by the Nazis included Communists, Socialists, Jehovah's Witnesses, and homosexuals. These groups were systematically rounded up and placed in extermination camps.

The Nazis deported millions of people from Poland and Western Russia for use as forced labor in German war plants, where they worked without adequate food, clothing, shelter, or medical care until they were dead.

About a half-million of Germany's Jews fled Nazi persecution between 1933 and 1939, as did two-thirds of Austria's 180,000 Jews. But there was little chance of escape for the nine million Jews of Central and Eastern Europe. When their nations were overrun by Hitler's armies in 1939, they became the victims of Hitler's murderous plot to annihilate Europe's Jewish population completely. In the end, an estimated six million Jews died in the Holocaust.

The Holocaust lasted until 1945 when the Nazis were defeated by the Allied powers. Hard evidence of this brutal regime's evil campaign against Jews and others was discovered and documented by Allied forces that retook Europe's Nazi-occupied countries and Germany itself.

Martha Gellhorn, United Press foreign correspondent and wife of novelist Ernest Hemingway, accompanied American troops and witnessed grisly scenes when our forces liberated Buchenwald in Germany. She wrote:

"There can never be peace if there is cruelty like this in the world. And if ever again we tolerate such cruelty, we have no right to peace."

The names of some of these camps live in infamy. Anne Frank died at Bergen-Belsen camp. Dachau was the first extermination camp. At Auschwitz, more than 1,000,000 Jews, Gypsies, Poles, Soviet POWs, and others were killed.

By the end of the War, the death camps system stretched from France and the Netherlands in the West to Estonia, Lithuania, and Poland in the East.

Toward the end of the War, many camps became sites for medical experiments, including eugenics, freezing prisoners to determine how downed pilots were affected by extreme exposure, and administration of lethal medicines.

A large proportion of prisoners in these camps died through deliberate mistreatment, disease, starvation, and overwork. Prisoners were transported in inhumane conditions by rail freight cars in which many died before reaching their destinations. The prisoners were confined to the boxcars for days or even weeks, with little or no food or water. Many died of dehydration in the intense heat of summer or froze to death in the winter.

So many died in these camps that disposal of their bodies became a major issue. After the bodies were stripped of usable clothing and shoes, some were burned in gigantic gas ovens, but most were bulldozed into giant trenches as their final resting places.

When Russian troops discovered Auschwitz eleven days after the Germans abandoned it, they found the remnants of a horrible nightmare: 348,820 men's suits and 836,515 women's dresses neatly folded. Pyramids of dentures and eyeglasses. Seven tons of women's hair.

As mentioned above, the largest groups of internees, both numbering in the millions, were Polish Jews and Soviet POWs.

In 1945, when the British forces entered the Bergen-Belsen camp, 60,000 prisoners were found alive, but 10,000 died within a week of liberation because of typhus and malnutrition.

Included among the most infamous Nazi concentration/death camps were:

- Auschwitz- Birkenau (Poland)
- Bergen-Belsen (Lower Saxony)
- Belzec (Poland)
- Buchenwald (Weimar, Germany)
- Dachau – Gross-Rosen (Bavaria, Germany)
- Majdanek (Poland)
- Neuengamme – Ravensbruck (Northern Germany)
- Uckermark – Warsaw (Poland)

Soviet POWs in German Camps

The camps established especially for Soviet POWs were called *Russenlager* (Russian camp). The Allied soldiers captured by Germany were usually treated in accordance with the Geneva Convention's rules for POWs. Although the Soviet Union was not a signatory, Germany was. Article 82 of the Convention required signatories to treat all captured enemy soldiers "as between the belligerents who are parties thereto."

Russenlager conditions were often worse than those commonly experienced by prisoners in Nazi Germany's concentration camps. These were camps where political or racially inferior prisoners were starved and/or worked to death. Thus, the common name was death camps.

Bergen-Belson, Auschwitz-Birkenau, Buchenwald, and Dachau were infamous examples of the death camps where *undesirables* spent the last few months of their lives. Hundreds of thousands of Soviet POWs died or were executed in Nazi death camps. Most of these were killed by shooting, but some were gassed.

In January 1942, Hitler authorized better treatment of Soviet POWs because the war had bogged down, and German leaders decided to use prisoners for forced labor on a large scale. The number of forced laborers increased from barely 150,000 in 1942 to the peak of 631,000 in the summer of 1944.

Many were dispatched to the coal mines. Between July 1 and November 10, 1943, 27,638 Soviet POWs died in the Ruhr area alone. Others were sent to Krupp, Daimler-Benz, or other companies, where they provided labor while often being slowly worked to death. The largest employers of 1944 were mining (160,000), agriculture (138,000), and in the metal industry (131,000). No less than 200,000 prisoners died during forced labor.

The Organization Todt was a civil and military engineering group in Germany, named for its founder Fritz Todt. The organization was responsible for a wide range of engineering projects both in pre-World War II Germany and in occupied territories from France to the Soviet Union during the War. It became notorious for using forced labor.

Most of the so-called *volunteer* Soviet POW workers were consumed by Todt. During the period from 1942 until the end of the War, approximately 1.4 million laborers were working for the Todt Organization.

Overall, 1% were Germans rejected from military service and 1.5% were concentration camp prisoners. The rest were POWs and compulsory laborers from the occupied countries. All non-Germans were effectively treated as slaves, and many did not survive the work or the War.

At the time, both the government and the people of Germany managed to tolerate this deplorable and immoral situation.

German War Crimes Against Soviet POWs

It is estimated that at least 3.3 million Soviet POWs died while in Nazi custody, out of a total of 5.7 million Soviet POWs in Nazi POW camps. This figure represents a total of 57% of all Soviet POWs and may be contrasted with 8,300 out of 231,000 British and U.S. prisoners, or 3.6%. About 5% of the Soviet prisoners who died were Jews.

The most deaths took place between June 1941 and January 1942, when the Germans killed an estimated 2.8 million Soviet POWs, primarily through deliberate starvation, exposure, or summary execution.

At least one million Soviet POWs had been released. Most were so-called Hilfswillige, volunteers for compulsory auxiliary service in the Wehrmacht. Five-hundred thousand fled or were liberated while the remaining 3.3 million perished as POWs.

By September 1941, the mortality rate among Soviet POWs was in the order of 1% per day. In winter of 1941, starvation and disease resulted in the mass death of unimaginable proportions. This deliberate starvation despite food being available led many desperate prisoners to resort to acts of cannibalism that was Nazi policy and was in accordance with the Hunger Plan developed by the Reich Minister of Food, Herbert Backe.

For the Germans, Soviet POWs were expendable. They consumed calories and, unlike Western POWs, were considered to be subhuman or *Untermenschen*. This term became infamous when the Nazis used it to describe non-Aryans as *inferior people,* often referred to as *the masses from the East*, that is Jews, Roma (Gypsies), and Slavs (mainly Poles, Serbs, and Russians). The term also applied to Blacks, Mulattos, and Finn-Asians.

Jewish people were to be exterminated in the Holocaust along with the Polish and Romani people and the physically and mentally disabled. According to the *Generalplan Ost*, the Slavic population of East-Central Europe was to be reduced in part through mass murder in the Holocaust, with the majority expelled to Asia or used as slave labor in the Reich.

These concepts were the essence of the Nazi racial policy.

The *Kommissarbefehl* (The Commissar Order)

The *Kommissarbefehl* was the written order given by the German High Command on June 6, 1941 just prior to the beginning of Operation Barbarossa, the German invasion of the Soviet Union. The order demanded that any Soviet political commissar, a supervisory military officer, be identified among captured troops and shot immediately. Those prisoners who could be identified as thoroughly Bolshevized or as active representatives of the Bolshevist ideology were also to be executed.

In the summer and autumn of 1941, vast numbers of Soviet prisoners were captured in about a dozen large encirclements. Due to their rapid advance into the Soviet Union and an anticipated quick victory, the Germans did not want to ship these prisoners to Germany.

Under the administration of the Wehrmacht, the German armed forces, the prisoners were processed, guarded, force-marched, or transported in open rail cars to locations mostly in the occupied Soviet Union, Germany, and occupied Poland. As with the Pacific War's Bataan Death March in 1942, the treatment of prisoners was brutal.

Soviet prisoners were stripped of their supplies and clothing by poorly equipped German troops when the cold weather set in. This resulted in death for many prisoners. Most of the camps for Soviet POWs were simply open areas with no housing, fenced off with barbed wire and watchtowers. These meager conditions forced the crowded prisoners to live in holes they had dug for themselves, which were exposed to the elements. Beatings and other abuse by the guards were common. Prisoners were malnourished, often consuming only a few hundred calories or less per day. Medical treatment was nonexistent, and an International Red Cross offer to help in 1941 was rejected by Hitler.

Some of the Soviet POWs were also used in experiments. In one case, Dr. Heinrich Berning from Hamburg University starved prisoners to death as famine experiments. In another instance, a group of prisoners at Zhitomir, Ukraine were shot using dum-dum bullets. These bullets, designed to expand on impact, caused the bullet to increase in diameter to resist over-penetration and produce a larger wound. Dum-dum bullets are generally prohibited for use in war.

Author's Note. Writing the words above was very difficult. Despite the high cost in terms of the lives of American fighting men and those of our Allies, it should be obvious to every decent human in the world today that the Allies were on the honorable and just side in the struggle against a cruel, brutal, and demented enemy.

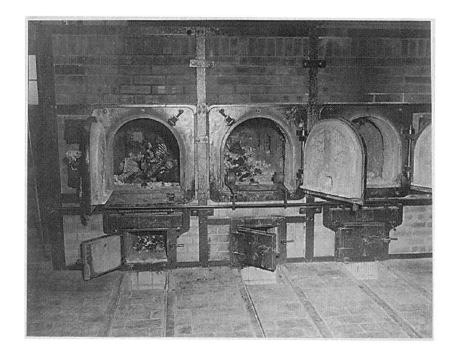

Bones still in the crematoriums in the German concentration camp at Weimar, Germany, taken by the 3rd U.S. Army. Prisoners of all nationalities were tortured and killed. *Photo from the National Archives. Identifier: 531260*

"There comes a point where a man must refuse to answer to his leader if he is also to answer to his conscience."

Ann Tusa, author of *The Nuremberg Trials,* published in 1984.

11. Retributive Justice

The Nuremberg Trials

Following the War, the top surviving German leaders were tried for Nazi Germany's crimes, including the crimes of the Holocaust. The trial was held before the International Military Tribunal (IMT) in Nuremberg, Germany, beginning on November 17, 1945.

Judges from the Allied powers, including the United States, Great Britain, France, and the Soviet Union, presided over the proceedings. The first trial addressed the wrongdoings of twenty-two major Nazi criminals. Later, the United States held twelve additional trials of high-level officials of the German government, military, the SS, medical professionals, and leading industrialists. Crimes charged before the Nuremberg courts were crimes against peace, war crimes, crimes against humanity, and conspiracy to commit these crimes.

One hundred and ninety-nine defendants were tried during the Nuremberg with 161 convicted. Thirty-seven were sentenced to death, including twelve of those tried by the IMT. Holocaust crimes were included in a few of the trials but were the major focus of only the U.S. trial of the *Einsatzsgruppen* leaders. These defendants readily acknowledged that they were responsible, but they were only following orders from their superiors.

The Nazis' highest authority, the person most to blame for the Holocaust was missing at the trials. Adolph Hitler had committed suicide during the final days of the War. Many more criminals were never tried. Some had fled from Germany to live abroad, including hundreds who came to the United States.

Trials of Nazis continued to take place in Germany and many other countries. Simon Wiesenthal, a Nazi hunter, provided leads for War crimes investigators about Adolf Eichmann, who had helped plan and carry out the deportations of millions of Jews. He was brought to trial from South America to Israel. Owing to the testimony of hundreds of witnesses, Eichmann was found guilty and executed in 1962.

Other indictments were handed down to twenty-four leading Nazi officials including:

- Hermann Goring (Hitler's Former Deputy)
- Rudolf Hess (Deputy Nazi Party Leader)
- Joachim von Ribbentrop (Foreign Minister)
- Wilhelm Keitel (Head of the Armed Forces)
- Wilhelm Frick (Minister of the Interior)
- Ernst Kaltenbrunner (Head of Security Forces)
- Hans Frank (Governor-General of Occupied Poland)
- Konstantin von Neurath (Governor of Bohemia and Moravia)
- Erich Raeder (Head of Navy)
- Karl Doenitz (Raeder's successor)
- Alfred Jodl (Armed Forces Command)
- Alfred Rosenberg (Minister for Occupied Eastern Territories)

- Baldur von Schirach (Head of Hitler Youth)
- Julius Streicher (Radical Nazi Antisemitic Publisher)
- Fritz Sauckel (Head of Forced Labor Allocation)
- Albert Speer (Armaments Minister)
- Arthur Seyss-Inquart (Commissioner for Occupied Netherlands).
- Martin Bormann (Hitler's Adjutant) was tried in absentia.

The Verdict of the Nuremberg Trials:

- The IMT imposed the death penalty on twelve defendants (Goring, Ribbentrop, Keitel, Kaltenbrunner, Rosenberg, Frank, Frick, Streicher, Sauckel, Jodl, Seyss-Inquart, and Bormann).
- Three were sentenced to life imprisonment (Hess, Funk, and Raeder).
- Four received prison terms ranging from ten to twenty years (Doenitz, Schirach, Speer, and Neurath).
- Three defendants were acquitted (Schacht, Franz von Papen, and Hans Fritzche).

The death sentences were carried out on October 16, 1946 with two exceptions. Goring committed suicide shortly before his scheduled execution, and Bormann remained missing. The other ten defendants were hanged. Their bodies were cremated, and the ashes were deposited in the Isar River. The seven major War criminals sentenced to prison terms were remanded to the Spandau Prison in Berlin.

International Military Tribunal for the Far East (IMTFE)

Despite the lack of consensus, General Douglas MacArthur, the Supreme Commander of the Allied Powers, decided to initiate arrests of those he considered to be Japanese war criminals. On

September 11, 1945, a week after the Japanese surrender, he ordered the arrests of 39 suspects, most of them members of General Hideki Tojo's war cabinet. Tojo tried to commit suicide, but he was resuscitated with the help of U.S. doctors.

On January 19, 1946, MacArthur issued a special proclamation ordering the establishment of the International Military Tribunal for the Far East (IMTFE).

The IMTFE, also known as the Tokyo Trial or the Tokyo War Crimes Tribunal, was a military trial convened on April 29, 1946 to try leaders of the Empire of Japan for joint conspiracy to start and wage war (Class A crimes), conventional war crimes (Class B), and crimes against humanity (Class C.)

Eleven countries (Australia, Canada, Chile, France, British India, the Netherlands, New Zealand, the Soviet Union, the United Kingdom, and the United States) provided judges and prosecutors for the court. The defense comprised Japanese and American lawyers.

Twenty-eight Japanese military and political leaders were charged with fifty-five separate counts encompassing the waging of aggressive war, murder, and conventional war crimes committed against prisoners of war, civilian internees, and the inhabitants of occupied territories. The defendants included former prime ministers, former foreign ministers, and former military commanders. In the course of the proceedings, the court ruled that forty-five of the counts, including all the murder charges, were either redundant or not authorized by the IMTFE Charter.

One defendant, Okawa, was found mentally unfit to stand trial, and charges were dropped. Two defendants, Yosuke and Osami, died of natural causes during the trial. All remaining defendants were found guilty of at least one count. Sentences ranged from seven years' imprisonment to execution.

Six defendants were sentenced to death by hanging for crimes against humanity, war crimes, and crimes against peace (Classes A, B, and C).

- General Doihara
- Koki Hirota, Prime Minister
- General Itagki, War Minister
- General Kimura, Commander, Burma Area Army
- Lieutenant General Muto, Chief of Staff, 14th Area Army
- General Tojo, Commander Kwantung Army (later Prime Minister)

One defendant was sentenced to death for war crimes and crimes against humanity (Classes B and C).

- General Matsui, Commander, Shanghai Expeditionary Force and Central China Area Army.

These above seven were executed at Sugam Prison on December 23, 1948.

Sixteen defendants were sentenced to life imprisonment.

- General Araka, War Minister
- Colonel Hashimoto, Instigator of the Sino-Japanese War
- Field Marshall Hata, War Minister
- Baron Hiranuma, Prime Minister
- Naoki Hoshino, Chief Cabinet Secretary
- Okinori Kaya, Finance Minister
- Marquis Kido, Lord Keeper of the Privy Seal
- General Koiso, Governor of Korea, later Prime Minister
- General Minami, Commander, Kwantung Army

- Admiral Oka, Naval Minister
- Lieutenant General, Oshima, Ambassador to Germany
- General Sato, Chief of Military Affairs Bureau
- Admiral Shimada, Naval Minister
- Toshio Shiratori, Ambassador to Italy
- Lieutenant General, Suzuki, President of Cabinet Planning Board
- General Umzu, War Minister

Other War Crimes Trials

More than 4,600 lower-ranking personnel were charged with conventional war crimes in separate trials held in eight different Allied countries. The charges covered a wide range of crimes including prisoner abuse, ill treatment of laborers, rape, sexual slavery, torture, and inhumane medical experiments.

Of those tried, 984 were sentenced to death, 475 received life sentences, 2,944 were given lighter prison sentences, 1018 were acquitted, and 279 were not brought to trial or sentenced.

Exoneration of the Japanese Imperial Family

The Japanese Emperor Hirohito and other members of the Imperial Family might have rightly been regarded potential suspects in the crimes described above. However, the Truman Administration and General MacArthur believed the occupation reforms they had in mind for Japan would be implemented much more smoothly if they were able to use Hirohito to legitimize their planned changes for Japan.

Nuremberg Trials: looking down on the defendants' dock. *Photo from the National Archives. Identifier: 540127*

"I wish to remember the millions of Allied servicemen and prisoners of war who lived the story of the Second World War. Many of these men never came home; many others returned bearing emotional and physical scars that would stay with them for the rest of their lives. With the deepest appreciation for what these men endured, and what they sacrificed, for the good of humanity.

Laura Hillenbrand, author of *Unbroken,* published in 2010.

12. POWs in Film and Television

Movies with Storylines about POWs

During the War, movie theaters showed newsreels featuring the latest progress of the War in Europe and the Pacific. All Americans were very interested in that news, because most had fathers, uncles, brothers, and cousins fighting the Germans or the Japanese at the time. Hollywood movies featured storylines about the War, including POWs and their camps. Below are important films related to POWs.

1943. THE CROSS OF LORRAINE
French POWs escape from a German prison camp and join the French Resistance. The title is the symbol of the French Resistance and the Free French Forces chosen by Charles de Gaulle in 1942. Starring Jean-Pierre Aumont and Gene Kelly.

1944. THE PURPLE HEART
Based on the trial and subsequent execution of eight U.S. airmen who were part of the Doolittle Raid on Japan. After being shot down, they took temporary refuge among the Chinese villagers, were captured by the Japanese, and executed. Brave and patriotic movie. Starring Dana Andrews, Richard Conte, and Farley Granger.

1950. THE WOODEN HORSE
True events of an escape attempt made by POWs in the German prison camp Stalag Luft III. The *wooden horse* in the title of the film is a piece of exercise equipment the prisoners used to conceal their escape attempt. This POW camp was where the real events included in the film *The Great Escape* took place, albeit a different compound. Starring Leo Glenn, David Tomlinson, and Anthony Steel.

1950. THREE CAME HOME
Post-war movie based on a book of the same title written by Agnes Newton Keith. Depicts the author's life in North Borneo in the period immediately before the Japanese invasion in 1942 and her subsequent imprisonment and suffering when she was interned in Batu Lintang in Kuching, Sarawak. Camp was liberated in 1945. Starring Claudette Colbert, Patri Knowles, and Sessue Hayakawa.

1953. STALAG 17
Classified as a comedy-drama by its reviewers. Tells of a group of American airmen held in a German POW camp. One of their number is an informant. Suspicions run high as the designated villain continues his shifty ways. Starring William Holden, Don Taylor, and Otto Preminger.

1955. THE COLDITZ STORY
British POWs are forced to assist their German captors to transform Colditz Castle into a high-security POW camp called Oflag IV-C. Colditz was designed to hold Allied POWs who had escaped from less secure camps in the past. Starring John Mills, Eric Portman, and Christopher Rhodes.

1956. A MAN ESCAPED
Based on the memoir of Andre Devigny, a member of the French Resistance, who escapes from the German Montluc prison. He is captured but escapes a second time to rejoin the Resistance. Starring Francois Leterrier and Charles Le Clainche.

1957. THE BRIDGE ON THE RIVER KWAI
Epic war film directed by David Lean. Uses the historical setting of the British POWs' construction of the Burma Railroad, 1942-1943. Film won seven Academy Awards. Highly honored and considered one of the finest War movies ever made. Starring William Holden, Jack Hawkins, Alec Guinness, and Sessue Hayakawa.

1957. THE ONE THAT GOT AWAY
Luftwaffe fighter pilot, Franz von Werra, is shot down during the Battle of Britain. He wagers with his RAF interrogator at the POW reception center that he will escape within six months. His many attempted escapes make for an interesting story. Starring Hardy Kruger, Michael Goodliffe, and Colin Gordon.

1959. DANGER WITHIN
A British war film set in a POW camp in Northern Italy during the summer of 1943. A combination of POW escape drama and whodunnit, based on the 1952 novel, *Death in Captivity,* by Michael Gilbert, who actually had been a POW in an Italian camp during the War. Starring Richard Todd and Michael Wilding.

1961. THE LONG AND THE SHORT AND THE TALL
Set during the 1942 Malayan Campaign. A seven-strong British sonic-deception unit hides from Japanese in an abandoned mine. The crew fights off Japanese to load the mine with explosives. Daring storyline. Starring Richard Todd and Laurence Harvey.

1963. THE GREAT ESCAPE
Based on Paul Brickhill's nonfiction book of the same title. A first-hand account of a mass escape of British and American prisoners from German POW Stalag Luft III in the province of Lower Silesia, Nazi Germany. Actual events are depicted in this fictionalized version, the best POW camp escape movie. I would hate to tell you how many times I have watched this gem. Starring Steve McQueen, James Garner, and Richard Attenborough.

1965. KING RAT
Corporal King is an anomaly in the Japanese POW camp. One of a handful of Americans among the British and Australian inmates who thrives by conniving and black-market enterprises. When inmates learn that Japan has surrendered, everyone rejoices, except Corporal King who mourns the loss of this thriving business. Starring George Segal, Tom Courtenay, and Patrick O'Neal.

1965. VON RYAN'S EXPRESS
A group of Allied POWs conducts a daring escape by hijacking a freight train and fleeing through German-occupied Italy and into Switzerland. One of Frank Sinatra's most successful films. Starring Frank Sinatra, Trevor Howard, Raffaella Carra, and Brad Dexter.

1969. HANNIBAL BROOKS
British-American War comedy. A POW attempts to escape from Nazi Germany to Switzerland, accompanied by an Asian elephant. Based on the true story of an American POW who spent his

captivity taking care of Asian elephants at the Munich Zoo. Starring Oliver Reed and Michael J. Pollard.

1970. THE FIFTH DAY OF PEACE

Based on the true story of two German sailors, both executed for desertion after being found guilty of cowardice by fellow POWs. The sentence was carried out by German POWs who were interned in a Canadian POW camp in Amsterdam. Starring Richard Johnson and Franco Nero.

1970. THE McKENZIE BREAK

A British intelligence officer investigates disturbances in German POW camp in Scotland. While the investigation is in full swing, a German officer leads his 28-man escape party to rendezvous with a German U-boat arranged to meet them on the nearby shoreline. Starring Brian Keith, Helmut Griem, and Ian Hendry.

1978. SUMMER OF MY GERMAN SOLDIER

Twelve-year-old Patty Bergen lives in a small Georgia town with her family. During the war, a German POW camp is established on the outskirts of town. One of the young German POWs escapes and is befriended by Ms. Bergen. Their relationship keeps this story quite interesting. Starring Kristy McNichol, Bruce Davison, and Esther Rolle.

1979. ESCAPE TO ATHENA

In 1944, Allied prisoners in a German POW camp on an unnamed Greek island are forced to excavate ancient artifacts for the camp commander, a former Austrian antiques dealer. He sends these items to his sister living in Switzerland. The story traces these valuable artifacts to America. Starring Roger Moore and Telly Savalas.

1981. ESCAPE TO VICTORY
An American sports War film, starring a number of prominent American sports stars. Allied POWs in a German camp play an exhibition match of football (soccer) against a German team. Starring Sylvester Stallone and Michael Caine.

1983. MERRY CHRISTMAS, MR. LAWRENCE
Relationships of four men in a Japanese POW camp during the War. The first is a British officer, the second the Japanese camp commander, the third a British officer who speaks Japanese fluently, and the fourth is the main character. As it is apparent the allies will win the War, the four men experience difficulty reconciling their differences. Starring David Bowie, Tom Conti, Ryuichi Sakamoto, and Jack Thompson.

1987. ESCAPE FROM SOBIBOR
Story of the mass escape of Jewish prisoners from Camp Sobibor, a German extermination camp. Of the 600 Jewish inmates in the camp awaiting their turn in the gas chamber, roughly 300 escaped. Starring: Alan Arkin, Joanna Pacula, and Rutger Hauer.

1987. EMPIRE OF THE SUN
Story of a young boy who transitions from living in a wealthy British family in Shanghai to becoming a POW in a Japanese internment camp. He compensates for his losses by appealing to his Japanese captors in most ingenious ways. Starring Christian Bale, John Malkovich, Miranda Richardson, and Nigel Havers.

1990. BLOOD OATH
Australian film based on real-life trial of Japanese soldiers for War crimes committed against Allied POWs on the island of Ambon in the Netherlands East Indies (Indonesia) in 1942. Starring Bryan Brown, George Takel, and Terry O'Quinn.

1997. PARADISE ROAD

A group of English, American, Dutch, and Australian women are imprisoned by the Japanese in Sumatra during World War II. They bond and organize a vocal orchestral group to fill their time. Their use of this bonding experience to endure the rigors of imprisonment is the film's central theme. Starring Glenn Close, Frances McDormand, and Pauline Collins.

2002. HART'S WAR

Lt. Thomas Hart is captured by the Germans and transferred to Stalag VI-A where he cooperates with his German guards. After being released, when asked if he cooperated, he denies it. Later, his circumstances demand full honesty. Starring Bruce Willis, Colin Farrell, and Terrence Howard.

2005. THE GREAT RAID

In 1944, American forces close in on a Japanese prison camp holding about 500 survivors of the Bataan Death March. The film covers the dangerous resistance work by Nurse Margaret Utinsky who smuggled medicine to the prisoners. Starring Benjamin Bratt, James Franco, and Connie Nielsen.

2013. THE RAILWAY MAN

During the War, Eric Lomax is a British officer who is captured by the Japanese in Singapore and sent to a Japanese POW camp. There Lomax is tortured by the Japanese for having built a radio receiver from spare parts. His intent was to use the radio to entertain and boost the morale of his fellow prisoners. These recollections of this traumatic time in his life last forever. Starring Colin Firth, Nicole Kidman, and Jeremy Irvine.

2014. UNBROKEN

During an April 1943 bombing mission against the Japanese Island of Nauru, Louis Zamperini is a bombardier in a B-24 Liberator bomber. On a subsequent mission, his bomber is shot down. He and a fellow crewman survive for several days without food or water before being picked up by the Japanese and imprisoned in a POW camp on Kwajalein Atoll. This is just the beginning of an incredible story. Starring Jack O'Connell, Domhnall Gleeson, and Miayvi.

Author's Note. This movie was based on the bestselling book having the same title and was written by Laura Hillenbrand, who grew up with my children in Edgemoor, a residential community in Bethesda, Maryland.

2015. LAND OF MINE

A Danish-German film about German POWs sent to clear land mines in Denmark after World War II. Nearly half of the mostly young POWs were killed clearing the mines under the command of Danish officers. Starring Roland Moller and Mikkel Boe Folsgaard.

Television Series Set in a WW II POW Camp

Perhaps the best known and the most popular television series featuring POW storylines was *Hogan's Heroes.* The comedic show ran for 168 episodes, spanning six years from September 1966 to April 1971, on the CBS network. It holds the record for being the longest running television program. It was inspired by World War II.

"From affable to laughable, the portrayal of the figure Sgt. Schultz, a leading role in the popular movie and television series

(1966-71) about life in a German World War II POW camp. The comedic presentation defied the image of a German War machine that murdered six million defenseless Jews and savaged much of Europe."

The above was the opening paragraph of a long article by Tim Chavez in Nashville's newspaper, *The Tennessean,* in 2005.

On the first page of the article, the author includes two photos. One shows the leading players in the television series. The other is of two American soldiers, German POWs from WWII, captured at Ardennes. They'd been fed daily starvation rations of a slice of bread and a bowl of soup made from dried peas and unpeeled potatoes. Their bodies, shrunken to mere skeletons covered with skin, are ugly reminders of the fate of many American soldiers captured by the Nazis.

The stars of *Hogan's Heroes* were Bob Crane as Colonel Robert E. Hogan, who coordinated an international crew of allied POWs running a special operations group from the camp. Werner Klemperer played Colonel Wilhelm Klink, the incompetent commandant of the camp. John Banner played the bungling but lovable German sergeant-of-the-guard, Sergeant Hans Schultz.

The plot is set in fictional Stalag 13, located in an unspecified location in Southern Germany. The American POWs used the camp to conduct Allied espionage and sabotage operations via a secret network of tunnels that operated under eyes of the inept Colonel Klink.

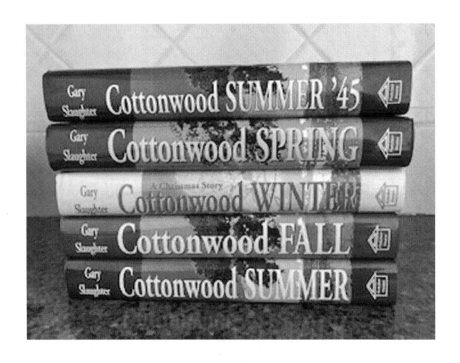

Gary Slaughter's five *Cottonwood* novels are used as supplemental high school texts. Each book contains a POW storyline and follows the War's progress during that season. Teachers view this series as an easy way for young people to study this period of American history. *Photo by Joanne Slaughter.*

13. POW-Related Excerpts from *Cottonwood* Novels

The five *Cottonwood* novels (*Cottonwood Summer, Cottonwood Fall, Cottonwood Winter, Cottonwood Spring,* and *Cottonwood Summer '45*) span the last five seasons of World War II and are replete with POW storylines. The series begins with the D-Day invasion in June 1944 and ends shortly after V.J. Day, the surrender of Japan, in September 1945.

Those last fifteen months strongly impacted America and the rest of the world. And the larger-than-life events provided a dramatic historical setting for these novels. Moreover, the world leaders who orchestrated these events included President Franklin D. Roosevelt, Sir Winston Churchill, J. Edgar Hoover, and Thomas E. Dewey, who are also characters in the *Cottonwood* stories. These men served as role models for the eleven-year-old home-front heroes, Jase Addison and Danny Tucker, who emulated, astounded, and ultimately befriended these four giants of history.

According to reviewers, the *Cottonwood* books are entertaining, comedic, heartwarming, gripping, and loyal to small-town values of mid-twentieth century America. But more importantly, they remind readers of the enormous sacrifices made by Americans as well as other peoples of the world during the War.

The story follows Jase and Danny as they go about life on the American home front. Jase and Danny follow the War's progress by listening to the radio and reading their newspapers. They engage in school activities and encounter German POWs along the way. Each novel features POW storylines.

Following are storylines excerpted from the novels.

From Chapter 16. *"Operation Matlock"* in *Cottonwood Summer*, published in 2002.

While some storylines involving POWs are fictional, the following is an actual incident that Billy Curtis (Danny Tucker) and I encountered one afternoon at our classmate Butch Matlock's (Ronnie Worthington) home.

On my way home from the dump, if Mrs. Matlock were not napping, I was accustomed to waving and exchanging warm greetings with her. I knew when she was on watch because, as I approached, I could see her muscular right arm propped on the windowsill. I didn't see Mrs. Matlock's arm that day, so I assumed she was napping.

While we chatted with Butch, I glanced up at her window. I was shocked at what I saw. A huge cloud of smoke rolled from her window. An eerie orange shade. What was I seeing?
Oh, no! "Fire! Fire!" I shouted at the top of my lungs.

I sounded the alarm again and again, jumping up and down under Mrs. Matlock's window. Danny and Butch were frozen. They stared at the window with their mouths open. We had to act fast. "Danny, quick! Scoot up to Pete's and call the fire department!" I ordered.

He snapped out of his spell and sped off in his wagon, his right leg whirling like an airplane propeller.

"Butch, keep yelling at your mother! You have to wake her up – before it's too late!"

With that, Butch let out a bellow that nearly burst my eardrums, **"MAW, WAKE UP! MAW, WAKE UP!"**

With Butch stuck in REPEAT mode, I ran as fast as I could toward the canning factory. At full speed, I flew around the east end of the building and leaped onto the loading dock near the infamous sauerkraut boxcar.

"Sergeant Rick! Mr. Don! Otto! There's a fire! Where are you?" I shouted as I pounded on the door marked "Retail Storage #2."

Don Paulus, the POW guard, opened the door almost immediately. Between gasps, I frantically outlined the situation. I concluded with a desperate plea,

"Mr. Don, we gotta get Mrs. Matlock outta that bedroom!"

Don didn't miss a beat. He ran back into the can storage area. I followed him admiring his ability to twist his awkward gait into such a brisk jog. When we rounded the corner, there they were, Otto and his crew of nine POWs.

"Otto! A fire! Bring the men! Quick!" Don ordered.

As we dashed toward the Matlock house, an explosion of fire erupted from the roof, spewing burning debris in all directions. A cloud of angry black smoke billowed skyward. Neighbors milled round and round in the street, frantically arguing about how best to rescue the imperiled Mrs. Matlock.

Three well-intentioned men attempted to quench the fire with garden hoses strung together from the spigot next door. But the angry fire ridiculed their paltry efforts by roaring furiously out of control through the now-gaping hole in the roof, just above and behind the sleeping Mrs. Matlock.

Otto and his crew sped to the scene, arriving well before Don and me. Just as Don and I reached Milford Street, I looked up to see a familiar, now reddened, arm protruding out of the upstairs window. I picked up the pace, leaving Don in my dust.

"MAAAWWWW!!!" Butch bawled at the first sight of his mother's wild-eyed face.

"HELP ME! FOR GOD'S SAKE! PLEASE, HELP ME!" she screamed.

Her eyes quivered with terror. We all felt helpless. Otto barked a series of short commands to his crew. They responded instantly with what sounded like a football cheer and then, without hesitation, they flew as a unit toward the front door, banged it open and disappeared through the wall of dense black smoke at the foot of the stairs. Otto followed his crew, in and up, yapping inspirational commands at their heels.

We were mesmerized by what we were witnessing. We stared blankly at the window. Suddenly, POW faces appeared there, around and above the panic-stricken face of Mrs. Matlock.

Magically, the form of Mrs. Matlock rose then very suddenly disappeared from sight!

Stomp! Stomp! Stomp! Scrapppppe! Stomp! Stomp! Stomp!
Bumpideebump! Bumpideebump!
Stomp! Stomp! Stomp! Crassssssssssssssh!
Bang!

The front door burst open. And, out came the POWs carrying the entire cot with Mrs. Matlock, in all her glory, clinging to her mattress. The POWs looked like ten pallbearers transporting a very alive, and very large, corpse.

Whish! Plunk!

Her ten Prussian footmen deposited Lady Matlock and soon-to-be twins, gently at that, right in the middle of Milford Street. Effortlessly. All in a day's work!

I looked up to the window where Mrs. Matlock had lain helpless only seconds before. The ravenous flames now gnawed hungrily at her windowsill. And, within seconds, they fully engulfed her former bedroom.

For once, Mrs. Matlock was speechless, overwhelmed by her emotions. Tears poured from her eyes.

The POWs broke into song. A rollicking German melody in the style of a school fight song filled the air. The smoke-blackened and slightly scorched rescuers bounced up and down, slapping each other wildly on the back.

Suddenly, the crowd of astonished onlookers roared with cheers and applause. They converged on the gleeful Germans, hugging them and pounding their backs. Otto's eyes filled with tears as he and his men garnered the uninhibited outpouring of gratitude and admiration from their American *enemies* from our neighborhood. Above the din, I heard an anxious plea, "Wait up! Cheese and crackers, Otto! Wait up!" It was Sergeant Rick Prella coming over the tracks, waving one arm and brandishing his Tommy gun in the other. I'd almost forgotten who was supposed to be guarding the POWs.

The sight of Sergeant Rick's U.S. Army uniform coming over the horizon incited yet another round of boisterous celebration. He was greeted by a wild flurry of cheers and immediately herded into the winner's circle where Don, Otto, and the grinning Germans stood, basking in our genuine affection.

Neighbors who arrived after the rescue were told what they had missed. They shook their heads in honest disbelief at the amazing news. In the midst of the festivity, Danny wheeled up and tapped me on the leg. He pointed with his thumb toward New Albany Avenue and the trio of neighborhood adults coming our way. They spotted Danny and me and threaded their way through the crowd toward us.

Before we could speak, the Riverton Fire Department pulled up with sirens screaming and diesels belching, warnings for us to stand aside. The crowd parted allowing the gigantic red fire engines to snuggle up to each other in the Matlock front yard. Like fleas from a wet skunk, the black rubber-coated firemen leaped to the ground, unreeled their hoses, and rushed for the rusty hydrant at the head of the block.

Within seconds, the hoses were fully charged and the firemen began the long process of drowning the Matlock fire and wetting down the nearby houses to prevent wind-blown, still-burning debris from setting them ablaze.

Amid a last round of applause, Otto and his crew allowed Sergeant Rick to reclaim his dignity by insisting that he march them back to the canning factory. A relieved Sergeant Rick appeared grateful for Otto's thoughtfulness.

Butch and his siblings now sat quietly in the street with their backs leaning against their mother's cot. They were a dazed and pitiful lot. Almost as an afterthought, a neighborhood teenager was dispatched to fetch an unsuspecting Mr. Matlock from his second shift job at the Ann Arbor Railroad boiler shop. He was in for a horrible shock!

From Chapter 1. "The Adventures Resume" in *Cottonwood Fall*, published in 2006.

As we made our way down Milford Street, we passed the construction site of the new house for the Matlock family. On temporary loan from the nearby canning factory, the same squad of German POWs that rescued Mrs. Matlock from the flaming house in June was now helping to rebuild the structure. Mrs. Matlock had given Danny and me credit for sizing up her plight and running to fetch the POWs in time to save her life.

She also gave us credit for convincing the *Riverton Daily Press* to print a retraction of their claim that the fire had apparently started as a result of Mrs. Matlock's smoking in bed. We knew for a fact that Mrs. Matlock never smoked or drank alcohol for that matter. After all, we had witnessed the passing steam locomotive shower the roof of the Matlock house with smoldering cinders. That was how the fire actually started.

"Hi, Otto!" we yelled.

Otto grinned broadly and waved from the roof where his squad was laying shingles. "Gut morgen, boyz!"

Otto Klump was our favorite POW. Initially, our warm feelings had to do with his access to bubble gum, a scarce wartime commodity for us boys. Not even Pete, our grocer, could get his hands on bubble gum. But the PX at Camp Riverton, where the POWs were interned, had a plentiful supply that Otto could purchase at prewar prices.

POWs could buy personal items using *canteen coupons* that they earned working in the factories and farms in our community. Danny and I had struck a standing deal with Otto to swap jars of sauerkraut from our family's supply for valuable packages of bubble gum. Everyone agreed it was a win-win proposition.

From Chapter 9. "Missing Danny" in *Cottonwood Fall*, published in 2006.

In Cottonwood Fall, *our neighbor, Junior Surtleif, returned from the War with an artificial leg. Unable to serve in the field, he has assumed an Army position at the nearby POW camp, Camp Riverton. He and Mr. Tucker, Danny's father, who had been wounded at Pearl Harbor, engaged in a conversation about German POWs.*

Mr. Tucker asked, "How do you like your new job, Junior?"

"Well, this job is a whole lot different than combat. I guess you could say that about any job. One thing the two have in common is the fine people. I really like working with the officers and men at Camp Riverton. Most have had combat experience and I respect that a lot."

Mr. Tucker nodded his understanding and agreement. "I was in the navy for a number of years before I picked up my shrapnel at Pearl Harbor. So I agree with what you're saying. The toughest thing for me would be to go into an outfit that wasn't squared away, that didn't follow good military order and discipline."

"That was a concern of mine as well. I'd heard stories about laxness at these camps and about the way discipline breaks down as guards get to know the individual POWs. There've been stories about POWs sneaking up and taking rifles from sleeping guards and hiding them as a prank.

"In some camps, lazy guards don't load their rifles because the bullets make their rifles too heavy! Not sure how I feel about this, but some POW camps provide German officers with drivers, cars, and permission to leave the base. Bound only by their word of honor not to escape, they can drive anywhere within a fifty-mile radius of the camp. I have to concede that, so far, not one has broken his word."

From Chapter 9. "The Battleground" in *Cottonwood Winter*, published in 2008.

The Cottonwood *novels follow the War with historical details of major events, like the Battle of the Bulge. These books are used as supplemental texts in American history classes in Michigan and Tennessee high schools. An interesting way for teenagers to study the War!*

The Battle of the Bulge was the last major offensive launched by Hitler's armies against the Allies during the Second World War. On December 16, 1944, the Nazi leaders directed the full force of three powerful armies against the farthest-advanced Allied unit, the American 106th Infantry Division that had fought its way eastward across Belgium and into Germany near St. Vith.

This massive German counteroffensive coincided with the coldest and snowiest winter ever recorded in the Ardennes Forest, the semi-mountainous and heavily forested region of eastern Belgium and northern Luxembourg. Because of the inclement weather and difficult terrain, Allied commanders considered the Ardennes to be the least-likely location for a German counteroffensive. Accordingly, they ordered their long front line to be thinly defended by only half the number of troops normally assigned to such duty. The 106th bore the brunt of the initial German assault.

Considering Germany's weakened state in late 1944, no one had expected Hitler to risk a major counteroffensive like the Battle of the Bulge. American bombers had devastated German cities, factories, and seaports. Since the early summer of 1944, Allied armies had retaken Italy, France, and the Low Countries. On its long march from Moscow to Berlin, the Russian Army had systematically crushed the frozen and exhausted Germans.

This counteroffensive was Hitler's last-ditch effort to drive a wedge between the Allied armies and cut off their access to reinforcements and supplies. Hitler's plan called for his armies in the Ardennes to advance westward to the Meuse River and then wheel northward to recapture the port of Antwerp. With this maneuver, he would encircle four of the Allied armies and cut them off from the sea.

Hitler was convinced that the alliance between the Americans, British, and French was weak and could not withstand a major loss on the field of battle. If his battle plan succeeded, he was certain that the Allies would settle for a negotiated peace on his western front. This would buy him the time needed to complete the development of his secret weapons, including nuclear bombs, long-range bombers, supersonic jet fighters, and intercontinental ballistic missiles. These weapons would ultimately ensure a German victory in the War.

At first, Hitler's plan did succeed. His Panzers, supported by 250,000 battle-hardened German troops, seized the initiative by encircling the inexperienced 106th Infantry Division near St. Vith and capturing more than nine thousand Americans. The Germans drove westward to within a few miles of the Meuse River southwest of Liege. In doing so, they created a *bulge* in the Allied line that was some 70 miles wide and 50 miles deep. This was the bulge for which the battle was named.

However, within a month, Hitler had abandoned all hope of winning the Battle of Bulge. There were several factors that contributed to this German defeat.

After first having underestimated the Germans' strength and determination, Allied commanders retaliated with massive reinforcements, equipment, and supplies to shore up Allied forces along the front line. This immense resupply effort was ultimately sufficient to overwhelm the remaining German forces. Unlike the Allies, the German army quite literally *ran out of gas*. Without fuel, members of Germany's vaunted Panzer Corps were forced to abandon their Tiger tanks on the battlefield and ignominiously walk home to Germany.

Despite heavy losses, the brave resistance by the 106th Infantry Division slowed down the Germans, costing them valuable time and resources. Because of this delay, the Germans lost the advantage gained during the first days of their Ardennes counteroffensive. In addition, the gutsy stand at Bastogne by the American 101st Airborne Division under General Anthony

McAuliffe deprived the Germans of this strategically important city for staging attacks against the stunned Allies.

Miraculously on December 22nd, the low cloud cover and fog, which had prevailed during the first several days of the battle, began to lift. This weather change brought the full force of American air superiority into the battle. On the next day, Americans began to counterattack the Germans. And, by January 16, 1945, the Battle of the Bulge ended with what was left of the German army in shambles.

In terms of American casualties, the Battle of the Bulge was the costliest battle of the War. We suffered 81 thousand casualties including more than 23 thousand captured and 19 thousand killed. The Germans suffered more than 100 thousand killed, wounded, or captured. And the Americans and the Germans each lost over 800 tanks.

From Chapter 14. "Stille Nacht" in *Cottonwood Winter*, published in 2008.

I have included interesting, but little-known, facts about the War. The subject of Kilroy always fascinated me.

NEAR THE END OF the war, Hitler developed a paranoid fixation on one insurgent who seemed capable of penetrating anything thought to be secure in Nazi Germany or its conquered territories. The Fuhrer personally ordered a massive manhunt for this super-spy with directions that the searchers must shoot to kill. The subject of Hitler's demented concern was none other than that ubiquitous rascal *Kilroy*.

Members of the underground resistance movements in France, the Low Countries, and Germany itself, plastered the Kilroy calling card on Nazi buildings and equipment throughout the Nazi-occupied areas. This action was designed to taunt the Germans and remind them that their enemies were never far away. While the image and slogan were nominally intended as graffiti and a prank, Hitler, fearing for his life, thought that Kilroy was out to get him.

Every time German commanders turned around, they were confronted by the Kilroy image, the oversize round head, long nose, and beady eyes staring at them over the doodled fence behind which Kilroy stood, grasping the fence with his pudgy fingers. And always the inscription, *Kilroy Was Here!*

It was downright disconcerting. There is no concrete evidence to verify how this Kilroy phenomenon started. It may have begun with James J. Kilroy who worked at the Bethlehem Steel Shipyard in Quincy, Massachusetts, as a shipyard inspector during the war. To show he had inspected the riveting on a newly constructed ship, he chalked the words *Kilroy Was Here!* on the bulkhead in question.

Later when American sailors and troops transited the Atlantic on ships inspected by Kilroy, they were mystified. All they knew was that he was there first. As a joke, they began placing those words, and later the image as well, wherever the U.S. forces landed or advanced through Europe, always claiming Kilroy's calling card was already there when they arrived.

During every operation, there was always one person who could be depended upon to leave the now-famous calling card. GIs began to think of Kilroy as a *super GI,* and his image and message began to show up everywhere they were camped or stationed. Yes, Kilroy became that super GI who always got there first.

GIs were challenged to place Kilroy's calling card in the most unlikely places. For example, during the Potsdam Conference, an outhouse was built for the exclusive use of the conference's principals, the Big Three (Truman, Churchill and Stalin). The first to use this facility was Stalin who emerged and, in Russian, asked his aide, "Who is Kilroy?"

When U.S. frogmen swam ashore on Japanese-held islands in the Pacific to reconnoiter the beaches prior to American amphibious landings, they reported seeing *Kilroy Was Here!* scrawled on make-shift signs and on enemy pillboxes. They left similar signs to greet the next GIs. This tradition continued throughout and following the War.

As the ultimate tribute to that super GI Kilroy, his image and message are engraved on the World War II Memorial on the Mall in Washington, D.C.

From Chapter 1. "Return to Riverton" in *Cottonwood Spring*, published in 2009.

The Conrad Hoffman storyline in Cottonwood Spring *depicts another type of prisoner during the War.*

"Is it my imagination or have I been talking to myself a lot lately?" Hoffman asked himself aloud as he admired his image in the full-length mirror.

He felt good to be in uniform again. Oh, how he missed the glory days back in New Jersey where he had been revered as a gifted protégé of their leader, the head of the German-American Bund.

And the crescendo at Madison Square Garden in 1939 had been ecstasy. He was really somebody back in those days, on top of the world and free of any ties to Michigan.

But now he was heading back home. It seemed strange, even surreal perhaps. When he looked at himself, fully shaved and still trim enough to fit into his old outfit, he experienced a sense of peace and serenity that he hadn't felt since the War started.

The War had changed everything. That's when the Bund he had worked so hard to build began to crumble. His colleagues and friends were rounded up like criminals. From time to time, he wondered what it would be like to be in prison with them. Sometimes, but not often, he even wondered what they thought about his abandoning them to protect himself.

Over the past six years, he continually reminded himself of how fortunate he was to have *obtained* the resources to finance his hurried departure. Oddly enough, he had not felt an iota of guilt about running away. He had fled because he feared arrest and imprisonment. His former Bund colleagues seemed to relish their collapse. As true zealots, they expected to be vindicated and rewarded in the end.

But Hoffman was no martyr. He was a pragmatist. An accountant by training, he relished order and control. His motivation for signing on was not religious fervor like the others. Hoffman sought wealth and power. He was convinced that the organization and its cause could help him meet his goals.

In truth, life had been hard for him since his departure. Like his old friends, he too was a prisoner of sorts. He had constructed his prison from fear and paranoia. Running from town to town. Working wretched jobs. Constantly looking over his shoulder in fear of discovery and arrest.

Shaking away those unpleasant thoughts, he pulled in his stomach, pushed back his shoulders, and saluted himself. It was just like the old days. He felt an overwhelming sense of pride and self-satisfaction. He focused on the grand purpose that had reactivated his enthusiasm. But suddenly he was brought back to earth.

"Conrad, do you have time for breakfast before you go?"

"Yes, Aunt Greta. I'll take time. It's a long drive so I'll need my strength. Yes, it's a very long drive."

As usual, her breakfast had been complete, nourishing, and tasty. He repacked his uniform, the incriminating papers he had hidden in Greta's basement in case they were needed to blackmail his former colleagues, and his cache of Bund money, the result of years of skimming off his share just as his leader Kuhn had done with Hoffman's help.

With this money, he would change his identity when he arrived in Chicago. He'd return to Michigan to settle some old grievances and visit some people, before disappearing for the last time.

Of course, for her own protection, his dear Aunt Greta would know nothing about this. In fact, she hadn't even asked where he was going in her car or how long he would be away. That's what he liked about Aunt Greta. Why couldn't his wife have been more like her?

From Chapter 8. "Danger in Riverton" in *Cottonwood Spring,* published in 2009.

"All right, gentlemen. The man's name is Sergeant Michael Shane. Six months before he was to graduate from Cal Poly with a degree in mathematics, the Japs bombed Pearl Harbor. He dropped out of school and enlisted. After boot camp, he was assigned to the 101st Airborne Division.

"Shane's very smart but he's no egghead. In college, he won several intercollegiate boxing titles. And he's a top marksman, one of a handful of field-qualified snipers with the 101st.

"Just prior to D-Day, he was one of the paratroopers dropped in behind the lines in Normandy. In the early action, Shane took a bullet through his calf and was assigned to watch over a dozen more seriously wounded men from his company until they could be evacuated.

"During the Waffen SS' Normandy counteroffensive, his position was overrun by Germans. He and the wounded were captured, thrown into boxcars, and shipped to a temporary camp near the Belgian-German border. For six months, he watched German guards brutalize the American POWs. Like the rest, he was systematically starved and tortured for no good reason.

"After nearly six months of starvation, beatings, and squalid conditions, he was rescued by the Americans. He was in pretty bad shape, but after a few weeks in an English hospital, he was shipped back to the States for reassignment.

"He reported to Camp Riverton about three weeks ago. After my first conversation with him, I knew he was trouble. I could see it in his eyes. Because his file contained no results of a psych evaluation, I ordered one myself.

"Within days after his arrival, he was into it with the Germans. Constantly complaining they were being coddled by their guards and by the Army's policies. He couldn't see why the POWs deserved -- using his terms -- their luxury food rations, their warm bunks, or their cushy jobs in the community. He ranted and raved about German POWs who were earning college credits from MSC professors when he had sacrificed his degree by dropping out to fight the blinking Germans.

"When he learned about Marie's sewing classes, he fumed about it for days. He told his bunkmates that no foolish female ought to be allowed inside the camp and that her very presence was a threat to good order and discipline.

"His language describing Marie became so outrageous POWs and guards alike complained about it. I warned Marie 10 days ago. Told her to stay clear of him. I was buying time until the psychiatrists from Camp Custer could examine him. I was confident we'd all be rid of him soon.

"By yesterday, I'd had it. I sent him off on temporary duty to fill in for one of three guards, watching over two dozen POWs working at a pig farm north of Frankenmuth

"There was no one living at the farm so the POWs and their guards were billeted in the big old farmhouse. Since there was no cook or ready source of groceries, guards and prisoners took their meals in Frankenmuth. A tavern there served genuine German food and plenty of beer in the bargain.

"I gave Shane a map, a jeep, and directions. He was *not* happy. He groused all the way out the door. He demanded that I shut down that sewing class and throw that -- you can guess what -- Marie Addison out of Camp Riverton by the time he returned, or else I'd be very sorry.

"Anyway, when he got to the pig farm, only one unguarded POW was there. He was suffering from the flu and had decided to skip the Sunday night meal at the tavern with the others. Shane huffed out of the farmhouse and headed for town.

"When he arrived, the tavern was filled with local German-speaking farm people, the two guards, and all the POWs.

Everyone was swilling down pitchers of beer and dancing to loud polka music. When the two guards saw him enter, they waved him over. He walked up to their table and told them to get the -- heck -- out of there or he'd clear the place with his tommy gun. They didn't take him seriously.

"A local woman came up behind him and put her hands over his eyes. According to witnesses, he spun around and slapped the woman across the face, he shook his fist at her, and yelled, 'I told you to get out of my camp! Do you understand that -- Miss Marie Addison? If I ever see you again, I'll kill you.'

"To make his point, he turned around and shot a burst from his machine gun at the table, killing two POWs and one of the guards. Then he ran out of the tavern, leaped into the jeep, and sped away."

From Chapter 15. "Back in Action" from *Cottonwood Summer 45*, published in 2012.

The two main characters from the Cottonwood *series, Danny Tucker and Jase Addison travel from Riverton, Michigan to Nashville, Tennessee in the summer of 1945. Their trip is to visit with their good friend JB who is spending the summer in Nashville, his original hometown. Jase, the narrator of the* Cottonwood *stories, relates an incident involving a POW.*

We boarded the West End bus well before its departure time. As a result, the two seats directly behind the driver were empty. As usual, Danny preferred the window, leaving the aisle seat for me. JB sat in the seat directly across the aisle from me.

Within minutes, the bus was nearly full. The passengers closely resembled those that we'd seen that morning. Young and old.

White and black. Military and civilian. Well-dressed and work-dressed. In short, it was another diverse group.

Just as the driver reached for the lever to close the door, a large man wearing a set of wrinkled, white coveralls ran down the sidewalk toward us and pushed his way through the door and onto the bus. Immediately I thought there was something odd about him. Danny must have felt the same way because he nudged me slightly with his elbow.

"Excuse me, sir. Your fare," the driver reminded the man. "You forgot to deposit your fare. It's ten cents, please."

"Eh?"

"Ten cents!" the driver repeated a little more loudly. This time he rubbed his first two fingers with his thumb, the international sign for money.

Something struck me about the man. Suddenly I remembered. Turning to Danny, I whispered, "German jackboots!"

He nodded his head in response. Silently his lips formed the letters, "P. O. W."

I slowly nodded my agreement.

I watched as the man moved to the back of the bus. Perhaps to be as far away from the driver as possible, he sat down next to an elderly black man in the last row of seats. I turned to Danny and pointed with my thumb toward the back.

Danny rose and looked for himself. Then he sat back down and concluded somberly, "Apparently he's not familiar with Southern customs."

"Jase, what's going on?" JB whispered.

I quietly related our suspicions about the last passenger. JB looked for himself. Then he nodded his agreement. "What'll we do?" JB whispered.

I pointed at JB and after that at the driver. He shook his head and pointed back at me. He was right. I knew what to say. So, I patted my chest and nodded in agreement.

Leaning forward, I tapped the driver on the shoulder. When he turned slightly toward me, I whispered my suspicions in his ear. The driver leaned into the aisle, took one look, and immediately reached out his window to beckon a police sergeant, standing on the sidewalk. When the officer came to the window, the driver whispered in his ear. The police officer whispered his instructions to the driver who nodded his head.

The driver left his seat and stood in the aisle. "Folks, I'm afraid I have some bad news. We're having mechanical difficulties with this bus and will have to change to another bus. I would appreciate y'all taking the same seats in the new bus as you have now. We'll unload, starting with the back row first. Then the next row -- you follow the back-row folks -- and so on. That's right. Thank you."

Among the first people off the bus were black passengers and our suspected POW. When the suspect stepped off the bus, he was immediately taken into custody by a contingent of Nashville's finest. They marched him off to a nearby squad car, pushed him into the caged-in backseat, and slammed the door.

Then the police sergeant returned and spoke to the passengers standing outside the bus, "Sorry for the inconvenience, folks. Y'all are free to re-board. There's nothing wrong. Thanks for your cooperation."

As the last of the passengers climbed aboard the bus, the police sergeant spoke to the driver, "Joe, I need you and those three boys to come down to the station. We'll make arrangements to get a substitute driver here as soon as possible."

We waited until the driver collected his jacket, lunch-pail, and morning paper. Then we followed him off the bus. When the police sergeant finished talking on his squad-car radio, he walked over to us and shook each of our hands. "Thank you, men. We've been on the lookout for this fellow for a number of days now. He escaped from Camp Forrest earlier this week. His name's Korff. Apparently, he's a bad actor.

"We focused our search efforts on Union Station and here at the bus exchange. But it looks like you young gentlemen are better at spotting wayward POWs than we are. I've called ahead -- I need you to come to police headquarters and tell your story to the chief."

Addressing the driver, he said, "You too, Joe."

Naturally we accepted his invitation. After all, we heroes were used to acclaim.

BY THE TIME WE arrived at police headquarters, word of our role in capturing the escaped POW had spread among the press corps. As we walked up the front steps, we were quickly surrounded by a dozen reporters and photographers. We were peppered with shouted questions and flashbulb bursts.

JB resembled a deer in the headlights. His eyes were as big as saucers. "JB, we've been through this before. Don't look their way. Just stare at the sergeant's back and keep walking. Soon we'll be inside. It's just like cutting through the defense in basketball."

Apparently, my advice to JB did the trick. He smiled and his demeanor changed to dead serious. I'd seen that look before, just before he burst through the opponents to sink the ball. He'd be fine.

When we arrived at the chief's office, we received a welcome we hadn't expected. The office was filled with high-ranking officers and one distinguished gentleman wearing a finely tailored suit and tie. There was also an army captain whose insignia I recognized as that of the U.S. Army Military Police.

"Gentlemen, I'm Chief Braddock. Congratulations on a job well-done. You've earned the unqualified respect and gratitude of the Nashville Police Department."

We each introduced ourselves as the Chief shook our hands. Then he turned to the well-dressed gentleman, "Mayor Stout, may I present Masters Addison, Tucker, and Bradford. And Mr. Joseph Curry."

"I'm honored to meet y'all," the mayor boomed, vigorously shaking our hands. "As you saw on the way in, members of the press are eager to meet y'all formally. But before that, the Chief and I would like to hear how you knew to alert the police. How did you recognize this escaped POW? Let's start with you, Mr. Curry."

The bus driver quickly deferred to us, informing the mayor all he did was listen to my whisper, deem it important enough to alert the sergeant, and pass the information to him.

"So, Master Addison, it was you who tipped off the driver. Is that right?"

"Yes, sir. But before I did so, I conferred with my friends, Danny and JB -- Masters Tucker and Bradford -- to make sure they concurred."

JB gave me a smile, silently thanking me for including him on our crime-stopper team. Aside from the acclaim he rightly earned on the basketball court, this was his first experience being a hero like Danny and me.

"Exactly why did you conclude this man was a German POW, Master Addison?"

"There were a number of reasons, Chief Braddock. First, he was wearing white coveralls that didn't fit him -- they were much too large. Also, he had his white coveralls on inside out. I figured he was trying to conceal something. And unlike the other men on the bus, he wasn't wearing a hat.

"When he got on the bus, he didn't know where to put his fare. And when the driver confronted him, he didn't seem to understand. I don't think he speaks English very well. Apparently, he doesn't know the value of our money either because he let the driver choose the correct fare from his handful of coins. That reminds me -- his hands were very clean and soft-looking. They weren't the hands of the worker he pretended to be. And he wasn't carrying a lunch-pail or a toolbox like other workmen we'd seen this morning on the bus."

"Master Addison, I'm impressed. Anything else?"

"Yes, Your Honor. He was unfamiliar with your custom of reserving the back of the bus for black passengers only. He sat down next to an elderly, black gentleman in the last row of seats."

"Very interesting."

"Most importantly his footwear convinced me that he was a German POW."

"Footwear? For goodness sake! What was he wearing that gave him away?"

"German jackboots! They're worn by POWs who are former members of the SS. These boots are the knee-length -- shiny, black leather -- hobnail boots. You've seen them in newsreels worn by storm troopers *goose-stepping* down the street in Nazi parades."

"Yes, I've seen them. You know a lot about this subject for such a young man."

Danny joined the conversation. "From our experience with former members of the SS, I'd guess that Korff refused to wear standard army-issue work shoes. The pride and arrogance of this group of POWs are well-known. After they're in our POW camps for a while, they put aside their pride, join the rest of their comrades, and enjoy the benefits of being a POW in an America-based prisoner of war camp."

"My goodness, Master Tucker. You certainly know a lot about this subject, as well."

Danny ignored the compliment and added, "If you check, I'll bet he was captured relatively recently -- probably in Sicily or Southern Italy."

Turning to the others in the room, the mayor announced, "Gentleman, I think we have just heard from experts on the subject of German POWs. Captain Isley, what's your opinion on what these young gentlemen have told us."

The MP captain replied, "I concur 100 percent with everything the boys said. They're right. Korff is a former member of the SS -- captured in Sicily. I suspect these boys are from a town that's home to a POW camp. Right, boys?"

We nodded our heads. "We're from Riverton, Michigan. Camp Riverton is a German POW camp just on the outskirts of town."

"You aren't, by chance, the boys responsible for capturing a number of escaped POWs from Camp Riverton? And wasn't one of you kidnapped by POWs on two different occasions?"

"That's us, Captain. I'm the one who was kidnapped -- twice. But I outwitted them -- both times," Danny announced, once again, inspecting his fingernails.

Chow is served to American Infantrymen on their way to La Roche, Belgium. 347th Infantry Regiment. *Photo from the National Archives. Identifier: 531241*

"It was in August 1944 when I stood in front of a shop in the POW Camp at Fort Lewis considering what to buy first: an ice cream cone or a bottle of Coca-Cola. The last ice cream I had been able to buy in Germany was years ago. But Coca-Cola? Never before. So, I decided to take both. I suddenly realized how extremely lucky I had been to be captured by the American army and not the Russian one."

Former German POW Lt. Günter Gräwe, an 18-year-old in August of 1944.

14. My Postwar Interactions with German POWs

During the course of my career as a corporate information technology consultant, I was retained to advise executives how to manage their organizations most effectively. Many clients were headquartered in Europe, affording me the opportunity to travel to numerous European cities. On some occasions, clients asked me to join them for lunch or dinner. Their purpose for spending time with me was to relate their experiences as POWs in America during World War II.

Much of the content of my *Cottonwood* novels relates to the experiences of former German military officers who spent time in POW camps in America. The stories below are examples of former POWs' experiences during their stays in America.

Saxon Chat

In 1972, as Product Manager for RMS (Brandon Applied Systems' *Resource Management System,* I flew to our London office to introduce RMS to the members of the staff. On my return flight, I was seated next to a friendly gentleman with whom I chatted for several hours during the long flight back to Washington. I noticed that he spoke with an unusual accent. I judged it to be a mixture of British and German. And I was right.

Later in the conversation, he explained that he was originally from Saxony, an eastern province of Germany. Owing to his strong loyalty to his provincial roots, he and his fellow Saxons had shared a general disrespect for Hitler and his Nazi regime. Nonetheless, he had been forced to join the German Army during the War.

During the Battle of the Bulge, he was captured by British forces and imprisoned in an English POW Camp for the duration of the War. Somehow, after the War ended, he managed to avoid being repatriated to Saxony. Instead, he remained in England, where he prospered as the owner of an import-export business that required him to travel abroad frequently.

When we reached Dulles Airport in Washington, we exchanged business cards and agreed to stay in touch with each other. Unfortunately, that never came to pass.

Later, I realized that his being a German POW was not unlike the many POWs that I observed at Camp Owosso as a young boy. It was indeed an interesting coincidence that I have never forgotten.

Lufthansa Airlines

Later in the same year, I was contacted by Hans Dirks, the Computer Center Manager at Lufthansa Airlines, headquartered in Cologne, Germany. His company was extremely interested in acquiring our OCS (*Operations Control System*), a component of our proprietary software package, *Resource Management System* (RMS). He wondered if I could arrange for him and a British consultant, Thomas Babbitt, who was advising him, to visit an OCS installation in Washington, D.C.

Because of my excellent working relationship with a local OCS client, the IT department of the Prince Georges County (PGC) government in suburban Washington, I assured Herr Dirks that I could arrange a visit.

The next week, I met the two potential clients at the Lufthansa gate when they arrived at Dulles Airport and drove them to a nearby hotel. The next day, they rented a car and met me at our Arlington offices. We spent the day at the PGC Data Center in Upper Marlboro. They were completely satisfied and, when we returned to the Brandon offices, Mr. Dirks signed a contract for OCS.

To celebrate the occasion, my wife and I hosted a dinner at our Chevy Chase, Maryland, home that evening. She had prepared a sumptuous roast beef dinner. I carved the roast and passed the dinner plates around the table. At the time, like many Americans, I consumed large quantities of beef, so my serving sizes reflected my standard.

Our two European guests, however, politely informed me that they could only comfortably consume a small portion of beef. While we thought it strange, we then remembered that European families were deprived of meat during the War years.

A few days later, I flew to Cologne to oversee the OCS installation. When I arrived at the Lufthansa Computer Center, Herr Dirks told me that his manager, Herr Duchterlein, the Vice President for Information Technology, would like to meet me for lunch. I was curious, so I gladly accepted the invitation.

After Herr Duchterlein and I were seated, he revealed in broken English, that during the War he had been a POW in a POW camp in Wisconsin. He excitedly described his time in America in the most glowing terms. It was quite apparent that he, like so many other POWs, truly enjoyed his stay.

During our two-hour lunch, he regaled me with tale after tale of his Wisconsin wartime stay. In turn, I shared my early experiences with German POWs growing up in Owosso. To me, the most amusing part of this exchange was Herr Duchterlein's continued use of American slang that was popular during the time of his internment. One of his terms has stuck with me over the years, *"Twenty-three, skidoo."*

For those not familiar with the saying, generally it referred to leaving quickly or being forced to leave quickly by someone else. Today we might say "Getting out while the getting is good."

"The endless procession of German prisoners captured with the fall of Aachen marching through the ruined city streets to captivity." Germany, October 1944. *Photo from the National Archives. Identifier: 541597*

American soldier with three of the 500,000 Germans captured at the Battle of the Bulge. *Photo from the National Archives. Identifier: 12010189.*

15. Americans Recall POWs in the U.S. during WW II

In addition to my interactions with German POWs, friends and associates have shared their experiences on this subject.

John Seigenthaler

After the publication of *Cottonwood Fall*, John Seigenthaler spoke at our WNBA (Women's National Book Association) meeting in Nashville. During John's talk, he shared his memories as a young man working side by side with German POWs. These POWs were employed by his father's construction company to build the Veterans Administration Hospital on White Bridge Road, not far from where Joanne and I now live in Nashville.

When John learned that I had just completed two novels replete with storylines about POWs in America during World War II, he was *very* interested. The next day I delivered copies of my first two *Cottonwood* books to his office.

A few days later, his secretary informed me that John wanted to interview me on his nationally syndicated television program, *A Word on Words,* described as follows:

When Seigenthaler closes each episode of A Word on Words with his signature signoff, "Keep Reading," he means it. Seigenthaler has been hosting the show and celebrating reading and writing for over 40 years.

In late January 2007, my interview was taped in the studios of WNPT, the PBS affiliate in Nashville. My wife, Joanne, watched the interview through a large viewing window and chuckled as the interview progressed. When John began to cite some of Danny and Jase's antics, he broke into near-hysterical laughter, requiring the cameras to be shut down until he regained his composure. Of course, I joined him, and together we shared a wonderful laugh-fest. His anxious producer, Jonathan Harwell, continued to glance at his wristwatch with alarm, but John and I simply carried on laughing, regaining our composure, and somehow managing to complete the interview.

As I write this more than a dozen years later, I find myself chuckling again about the uproarious time we had and how long it took us to complete that half-hour show. I cherish my DVD recording of the program. It rests here next to my keyboard as I write.

During the series' forty-year run beginning in 1993, a notable list of guests ranged from Ann Patchett to astronaut Alan Shepard, to new Nashville *author, Gary Slaughter.*

John Seigenthaler was the editor of *The Tennessean,* founding editor of *USA Today,* assistant to Attorney General Robert F. Kennedy, and chair of the selection committee for the Robert F.

Kennedy Book Award. He was a passionate advocate of the First Amendment and, in 1991, founded the First Amendment Center at Vanderbilt University.

Ruth Beaumont Cook

In Ruth Beaumont Cook's book, *Guests Behind the Barbed Wire,* she describes in great detail the reunion she organized for former German POWs who were interned in Camp Aliceville in Western Alabama. The reunion was held in October 1989 with many former POWs returning to America to attend. In fact, many of the returning POWs had not been *residents* of Camp Aliceville but had been interned in other POW camps in America during the War.

Ruth informed me that one of her reunion attendees had been interned in Camp Owosso. He proclaimed that he had enjoyed an extremely positive experience there. Hearing her story made me proud of *my* POW camp.

Ceacy Henderson Halley

Learn Nashville was a column for *The Tennessean*, written by George Zepp. On January 19, 2005, the column's title was *POWs Filled Labor Gap in Midstate during War.*

Mr. Zepp opened his column with a relatively long but informative quotation from *Ms. Ceacy Henderson Halley of Nashville.*

"For 40 years beginning about 1920, the J.B. Henderson family lived on a 508-acre farm situated along the Cumberland River, including Cornelia Fort Airpark. In the summer during World War II, German prisoners of War were brought in to work on the farm.

"As a little girl then, I remember my mother seeing to it that enormous midday meals were served to them. Apparently, they came from Camp Forrest in Tullahoma, Tennessee. It was all very secret.

"I have searched in the Tennessee State Archives and found only one newspaper article on this subject. What other information is available? "

Mr. Zepp told Ms. Halley that farmers and others in Midstate benefitted greatly from the German and Italian POWs in Middle Tennessee's three POW camps. He explained that POWs were used on farms all over the country. Farmers paid $4 per day for their services. The POW received a coupon worth $.90 per day, which he could use for treats, including 3.2% beer, at the POW camp commissary. POWs helped farmers raise and harvest crops, including tobacco, hay, onions, and corn.

His article also informed readers about many of the subjects that you have read in this book. In short, I was impressed with the content of his article. Back in 2005, not much had been written on this subject as compared with today.

Bob Jordan

Bob Jordan, my old friend from Owosso High School, was also acquainted with the POWs from Camp Owosso.

"My parents owned a farm on the corner of M-13 and Copas Road, two miles north of Lennon, Michigan. The W.R. Roach Canning Company in Owosso leased land from my parents on which they built a pea vinery. Area farmers brought sweet pea vines by the wagon-load to be shelled in a long-shed housing five or six large

machines that separated the peas from the vines. The POWs unloaded the vines and fed them into the machines and collected the shelled peas in large boxes, which were shipped to the Roach canning factory in Owosso.

"German POWs from Camp Owosso worked at the vinery. I was six years old at the time and would go down to the vinery and watch the wagons being unloaded and the peas being shelled.

"As I remember there were two or three Army guards and a foreman at the site. The POWs were housed in 16′x 16′ military tents.

"The only thing that happened that could be blamed on having POWs so close to our home was my brother's bike disappeared one night. It was later found in a ditch close to the POW tents. When the pea harvest was over, the POWs were gone. They never caused us any real trouble."

Margaret Bentley

Over the last two decades, I have worked closely with the *Owosso Public Library* that I frequented when I was a student in Owosso schools. Margaret Bentley, Adult Services Librarian, provided me with four similar POW stories from Kenneth Schroeder, Arnold Lundy, Norma Babcock, and Ed Hartley, who grew up on farms near Owosso. Their stories were very similar to that of Bob Jordan.

Margaret also sent me a fine piece written by Konrad K.P. Kreiten, who lives in Dülken, Germany, located in North Rhine-Westphalia. Mr. Kreiten was captured during the Battle of the Bulge near Liege by American soldiers and was shipped to America, where he spent a year in a German POW camp at Fort Custer, Michigan.

His remarks were very similar to those I heard firsthand from former German POWs during my later travels to Germany. He felt very fortunate indeed to spend the final days of the War in an American POW camp instead of joining his former comrades fighting the frigid winter War in Russia.

Joan Baker Linhard

Another Owosso High School classmate shared her POW experiences.

"I was born in February, 1935, and have memories about the POW camp out west of Owosso. Our father, Clarence Baker, was a farmer near Lennon, Michigan. He had a farm truck and he put benches in the bed for POWs to sit on. In the morning, he would go to the camp, gather five or six POWs, and take them to the various farms that raised sugar beets.

"Initially, he was concerned about how safe it was for the POWs to work in the fields. He wondered if he needed armed guards and, if so, how many?

"The first morning he went to the camp, he was surprised at how polite the prisoners were. And there was no big deal about guards. The camp only assigned one guard, armed with what my dad described as a squirrel gun. The guard rode with my dad in the truck cab.

"This was in November when the days were cold and the fields were muddy. Prisoners had to cut the tops off the beets, put the beets in a pile, and later load them into the truck.

"Their noon meal was a cheese sandwich that they brought from the camp. Then, my mother got involved. We had a large round

electric cooker similar to today's crockpot. While my dad was on his way to pick up the prisoners, my mother prepared hot food in her cooker - chili, stew, or soup. My dad would stop back at our house to get the cooker before heading to the beet fields. So, everyone had a hot meal at noon.

"Sometimes my brothers or I would ride along to get the prisoners, while Mom was fixing the hot food. I remember how the POWs were homesick, missing their families. One man said that he was walking home from work in Germany when he was snatched off the street and told, "You're in the army now!" He was never able to say goodbye to his family.

"After the war, the prisoners returned home. However, a couple of them contacted my parents to tell them how grateful they were for the hot food. They and their families needed clothes, so through our church, my mother collected used clothes in good condition, packed them in boxes, and the church paid for the shipping. One box went astray and, instead of going to the POW's family, it was delivered to a church in Germany."

In May 2017, Gary and Joanne toured the *U.S.S. Silversides* (SS-236), a Gato-Class World War II *submarine, docked in Muskegon, MI. Silversides* received 12 battle stars for WWII service and is officially credited with sinking 23 ships during the war. Gary spoke about his role in the Cuban Missile Crisis to the membership of the USS Silversides Submarine Museum.

Conclusion

The account of POWs in America and abroad is truly a unique and interesting element of World War II of which most Americans were - and today many still are - unaware.

Today, the World War II POW story in America and throughout the world continues being captured in the written word with numerous publications of biographies, autobiographies, and memoirs, as well as visually by the viewing opportunities of this subject in movies, TV series and documentaries.

Through my writing during the past two decades, I am extremely gratified to have had the opportunity to share information about the subject that has held my interest for my entire life.

The World War II Memorial in Washington D.C. is dedicated to those Americans who served in the armed forces and as civilians during the second world war. Fifty-six pillars and a pair of small arches surround a square and fountain. The memorial is located on the National Mall between the Washington Monument and the Lincoln Memorial. *Library of Congress, Prints & Photographs Division, photograph by Carol M. Highsmith [reproduction number, e.g., LC-USZ62-123456].*

APPENDIX A: Bibliography

Chen, C. Peter. "Discovery of Concentration Camps and the Holocaust." http://ww2db.com/battle_spec.php?battle_id=136

Cook, Ruth Beaumont. *Guests Behind the Barbed Wire. German POWs in America: A True Story of Hope and Friendship.* Birmingham, AL: Crane Hill Publishers, 2007.

Cowley, Betty. *Stalag Wisconsin: Inside WW II Prisoner of War Camps.* Oregon, WI: Badger Books, Inc., 2002.

Gansberg, Judith M. *Stalag U.S.A.: The Remarkable Story of German POWs in America.* New York: Thomas Y. Crowell Company, 1977.

Gargaro, Tom. "What Country Had the Largest Army in World War II?" https://www.quora.com/What-country-had-the-largest-army-in-World-War-II.

"German American Internee Coalition." https://gaic.info/internment-camps/united-states-army-internment-facilities/

Heitmann, John A. Ph.D.: "Enemies Are Human." *Dayton Christian-Jewish Dialogue* (May 10, 1998).

"Hitler Youth." http://www.historyplace.com/worldwar2/hitleryouth/hj-boy-soldiers.htm.

Kozak, Warren. Japanese POW Camps during World War Two. *Curtis LeMay: Strategist and Tactician. Washington DC: Regnery Publishing, 2009.*

Krammer, Arnold. *Nazi Prisoners of War in America*. Lanham, MD: Scarborough House, 1996.

Kupsky, Gregory. "To Win Our War with Butter and Beefsteaks: Camp Crossville and the Treatment of Axis Prisoners." http://usgerrelations.traces.org/2003conference.gkupsky.html

"Liberation of the Nazi Concentration Camps 1933-1945." http://history.sandiego.edu/WW2Timeline/camps.html

Mason, Amanda. "5 Stories of Real-Life Escape Attempts by Allied POWs." (February 6, 2018). https://www.iwm.org.uk/history/5-stories-of-real-life-escape-attempts-by-allied-prisoners-of-war

"Owosso Prisoner of War Camp." https://www.mysdl.org/local-history/owosso-pow-camp

"Owosso Speedway and Prisoner of War Camp". http://www.shiawasseehistory.com/prison.html

Peterson, Michael: "Bound by Her Secret History." *The Argus-Press* (January 10, 2010).

Philibert-Ortega, Gena. "Little-known WWII Facts: German POWs in the U.S." https://blog.genealogybank.com/little-known-wwii-facts-german-pows-in-the-u-s.html

"Prisoners in Paradise." https://www.prisonersinparadise.com/history/

"Prisoners of War of the Japanese 1939-1945." https://www.forces-war-records.co.uk/prisoners-of-war-of-the-japanese-1939-1945

Roberts, Jeff. "POW Camps in World War II." The University of Tennessee Press, Online Edition 2002-2018. https://tennesseeencyclopedia.net/entries/pow-camps-in-world-war-ii.

Robin, Ron. *The Barbed-Wire College: Reeducating German POWs in the United States during World War II*. Princeton NJ: Princeton University Press, 1995.

Taylor, David A. "During WWII, the US Saw Italian Americans as a Threat to Homeland Security." https://www.smithsonianmag.com/history/italian-americans-were-considered-enemy-aliens-world-war-ii-180962021

"The Nuremberg Trials." https://encyclopedia.ushmm.org/content/en/article/the-nuremberg-trials

"The Treatment of Soviet POWs: Starvation, Disease, and Shootings." (June 1941-January 1942). https://encyclopedia.ushmm.org/content/en/article/the-treatment-of-soviet-pows-starvation-disease-and-shootings-june-1941january-1942

Windsor, Carol J.: "Owosso Speedway Quieter as a POW Camp in 1944." *The Flint Journal* (September 4, 1973).

Wright, Jerry: "For POWs at Owosso, Farm Work Sometimes Provided Benefits." *The Flint Journal* (May 25, 1986).

.

The American Red Cross played a vital role in POW life during WWII, particularly in Europe, where more than twenty-seven million parcels were distributed to U. S. and Allied prisoners of war. *Photo from the National Archives: Identifier: 516324.*

APPENDIX B: Index

Harvesting bumper crop for Uncle Sam. Movie star Rita Hayworth sacrificed her bumpers for the duration. Besides setting an example by turning in unessential metal car parts, Miss Hayworth has been active in selling war bonds." 1942. 208-PU-91B-5. *Photo from the National Archives. Identifier: 535932.*

U.S.S. Shaw exploding during the Japanese air raid on Pearl Harbor on December 7, 1941. *Photo from the National Archives. Identifier: 520590.*

APPENDIX C: Historical Events of World War II

The *Cottonwood* series of five novels is an historically detailed and accurate account of World War II. The following inventory covers

- Major events prior to World War II not covered in the series,
- World War II events covered in the *Cottonwood* books, and
- Major war events following the fifth *Cottonwood* book.

The *Cottonwood* series is approved for use as a supplemental history textbook in Michigan's Shiawassee County Schools and in Tennessee's Williamson County Schools. It is also incorporated into the Foreign Student Orientation program at Michigan State University.

Many adults who grew up during World War II enjoy a nostalgic trip through their past and sharing the adventure with their grandchildren.

Prior to *Cottonwood Summer*

1939
September 1 - Germany invades Poland to start World War II.
September 3 - Britain, France, Australia, and New Zealand declare War on Germany.

1940
June 14 - Germany launches the airborne Blitz against England.
September 27 - Axis pact signed by Germany, Japan, and Italy.
November 5 - Franklin D. Roosevelt reelected President.

1941
December 7 - Japan bombs Pearl Harbor.
December 8 - America declares war on Japan.

December 10 - Japan invades Philippines.
December 11 - Germany declares War on America.

1942
February 22 - Roosevelt orders MacArthur out of Philippines.
March 11 - MacArthur leaves Corregidor, pledging to return.
April 1 - Japanese-Americans sent to relocation centers in U.S.
April 18 - Doolittle conducts surprise B-25 raid on Tokyo.
May 8 - American forces defeat Japanese in Battle of Coral Sea.
June 5 - American forces defeat Japanese in Battle of Midway.
August 7 - Americans' first amphibious landing on Guadalcanal.
November 8 - Americans invade North Africa.

1943
May 13 - German and Italian troops surrender in North Africa.
July 9 - Allies land in Sicily.

1944
January 22 - Allies land at Anzio in Italy.
May 19 - Allies capture Monte Casino in Italy.

During *Cottonwood Summer*

1944
June 6 - D-Day: Allies land at Normandy in Northern France.
June 13 - First German V-1 attack on Britain.
June 19 - Americans down 220 Japanese planes in Marianas.
July 3 - Battle of the Hedgerows in Normandy continues.
July 20 - Assassination attempt on Hitler fails.
August 25 - Allies liberate Paris.

During *Cottonwood Fall*

<u>1944</u>
September 4 - Allies liberate Antwerp and Brussels.
September 13 - U.S. troops reach the Siegfried Line.
September 17 - Operation Market Garden begins.
October 14 - Allies liberate Athens. Rommel commits suicide.
October 20 - U.S. Sixth Army invades Leyte in the Philippines.
October 21 - Germans surrender at Aachen in Germany.
October 25 - 1st Kamikaze attack on U.S. ships in Leyte Gulf.
November 7 - Roosevelt defeats Dewey for U.S. President.

During *Cottonwood Winter*

<u>1944</u>
December 16 - Germans launch Battle of the Bulge.
December 17 - Waffen SS murder 81 U.S. POWs at Malmedy.
December 26 - Patton takes command of Bastogne in Belgium.

<u>1945</u>
January 9 - U.S. Sixth Army invades Lingayen Gulf on Luzon.
January 11 - U. S. air raid against Japanese bases in Indochina.
January 17 - German withdrawal from Ardennes complete.
January 17 - Soviets capture Warsaw.
January 26 - Soviets liberate Auschwitz.
January 28 - The Burma Road is reopened.
February 4 - Roosevelt, Churchill, and Stalin meet at Yalta.
February 16 - U.S. troops recapture Bataan.
February 19 - U.S. Marines invade Iwo Jima, 650 miles from Tokyo.

During *Cottonwood Spring*

<u>1945</u>
March 2 - U.S. troops recapture Corregidor in Manila Bay.
March 3 - U.S. and Filipino troops take Manila.
March 9 - Tokyo firebombed by 279 B-29s.
March 20 - British troops liberate Mandalay, Burma.
April 1 - Allies discover stolen Nazi art and wealth in salt mines.
April 1 - U.S. Tenth Army invades Okinawa, a Japanese state.
April 7 - B-29s fly 1st fighter-escorted attack against Japan.
April 7 - U.S. sinks battleship *Yamato* to foil attack on Okinawa.
April 12 - Roosevelt dies, succeeded by Harry S. Truman.
April 12 - Allies free camps at Buchenwald and Bergen-Belsen.
April 21 - Soviets reach Berlin.
April 28 - Italian partisans capture and hang Mussolini.
April 30 - Adolph Hitler commits suicide.
May 7 - German forces surrender unconditionally to Allies.
May 8 - Victory in Europe Day (V.E. Day).
May 9 - SS Reichsfuhrer Heinrich Himmler commits suicide.
May 20 - Japanese begin withdrawing troops from China.
May 25 - U.S. approves Operation Olympic to invade Japan.

During *Cottonwood Summer '45*

<u>1945</u>
June 9 - Japan announces that it will fight to the very end.
June 18 - Japanese resistance ends in Mindanao, Philippines.
June 22 - Japanese resistance ends on Okinawa.
July 5 - Liberation of Philippines declared.
July 10 - 1,000 Allied bomber raids against Japan begin.
July 14 - 1st U.S. Naval bombardment of Japanese home islands.
July 16 - 1st U.S. atomic bomb, *Fat Boy,* is successfully tested.
July 21 - Truman approves atomic bombs be used against Japan.
July 23 - French Marshall Pétain goes on trial for treason.

July 26 - Atlee succeeds Churchill as Prime Minister of Britain.

July 26 - *Little Boy* is unloaded at Tinian Island in South Pacific.

July 26 - The Potsdam Declaration demands Japan's surrender.

July 28 - U.S. B-25 bomber crashes into Empire State Building.

July 28 - Japan rejects Potsdam Declaration.

July 29 - Japanese submarine sinks *USS Indianapolis* (880 crew).

August 6 - *Little Boy* dropped on Hiroshima from a B-29.

August 8 - U.S.S.R. declares War on Japan. Invades Manchuria.

August 8 - Americans capture Mariana Islands

August 9 - 2nd atomic bomb, *Fat Man*, dropped on Nagasaki.

August 9 - Emperor Hirohito decides to seek peace with Allies.

August 14 - Japanese agree to unconditional surrender.

August 14 -MacArthur heads Allied occupation forces in Japan.

August 27 - B-29s drop supplies to Allied POWs in China.

August 29 - U.S. troops begin occupation of Japan.

August 30 - The British reoccupy Hong Kong.

After *Cottonwood Summer '45*

September 2 - Japanese sign surrender on board *USS Missouri*.

September 3 - Allies accept Japanese surrender of Philippines.

September 4 - Japanese troops on Wake Island surrender.

September 5 - British land in Singapore.

September 8 - MacArthur arrives in Tokyo.

September 9 - Japanese in Korea surrender.

September 13 - Japanese in Burma surrender.

October 24 - United Nations charter ratified by England, France, China, Soviet Union, and United States.

APPENDIX D: Photographic Scenes from World War II

On June 22, 1940, officials of Nazi Germany signed an armistice with the French Third Republic. On June 23rd, Adolf Hitler celebrated the German victory over France with a tour of Paris. *Photo from the National Archives. Identifier: 540179.*

This typical, inspirational poster during World War II was published and distributed by the War Production Co-Ordinating Committee. Color poster by J. Howard Miller. *Photo from the National Archives. Identifier: 535413.*

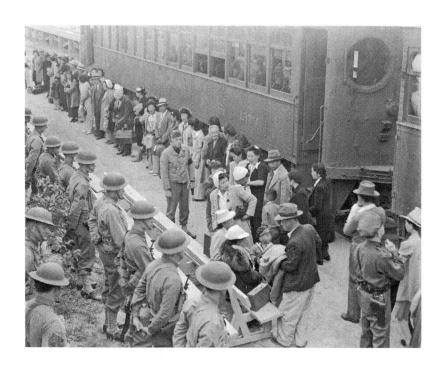

Beginning on April 1, 1942, Japanese-Americans were transported by train to relocation internment camps in the American West and the Southwest. On April 5, 1942, persons of Japanese ancestry arrived at the Santa Anita Assembly Center in San Pedro. Evacuees lived at this center at the former Santa Anita race track before being moved inland to relocation centers. *Photo from the National Archives. Identifier: 537040.*

In 1942 with American men serving in the military, women worked in shipyards constructing U.S. Navy warships. Here they are working as riveters for the Marinship Corporation. *Photo from the National Archives. Identifier: 522889.*

Jewish civilians from the Warsaw Ghetto are escorted by Nazi troops to concentration/death camps after the German invasion and conquest of Poland. Copy of a German photograph taken during the destruction of the Polish ghetto in 1943. *Photo from the National Archives. Identifier: 540124.*

Sixteen-inch guns of the U.S.S. Iowa firing during battle drill in the Pacific, ca. 1943. *Photo from the National Archives. Identifier: 520626.*

On April 17, 1943, Coast Guardsmen on the deck of the U.S. Coast Guard Cutter Spencer watch the explosion of a depth charge that blasted a Nazi U-boat's hope of breaking into the center of a large convoy, sinking U-175. *Photo from the National Archives. Identifier: 513166.*

A PT marksman draws a bead with his 50-caliber machine gun on his boat off New Guinea in July 1943. *Photo from the National Archives. Identifier: 520621.*

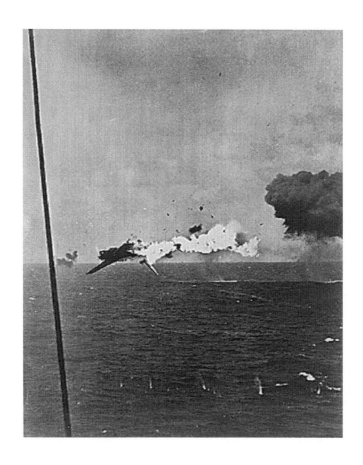

On December 4, 1943, a Japanese torpedo bomber explodes in the air after a direct hit by a 5″ shell from U.S. aircraft carrier, *U.S.S. Yorktown*, as it attempted an unsuccessful attack on the carrier. Alfred N. Cooperman. *Photo from the National Archives. Identifier: 520751.*

Under heavy Nazi machine-gun fire, American troops leave the ramp of an American landing boat and make an amphibious landing on the coast of Normandy in northern France during the D-Day Invasion on June 6, 1944. Robert F. Sargent. *Photo from the National Archives. Identifier: 513173.*

American Army medics treating a wounded Army soldier during the Normandy Invasion in France, 1944. *Photo from the National Archives. Identifier: 535973.*

Two U.S. officers plant the first American flag on Guam eight minutes after U.S. Marines and Army assault troops landed on the Central Pacific island on July 20, 1944. *Photo from the National Archives. Identifier: 532532.*

Following the liberation of Paris, American troops of the 28th Infantry Division march down the Champs Elysees, Paris, in the Victory Parade on August 29, 1944. *Photo from the National Archives. Identifier:* 535975.

In September 1944, parachutes open overhead as waves of paratroops land in Holland during operations by the 1st Allied Airborne Army as they march eastward toward Nazi Germany. *Photo from the National Archives. Identifier: 531392.*

On September 9, 1944 during the invasion of Belgium, American soldiers of the 60th Infantry Regiment advance into a Belgian town under the protection of an American tank. Later in the month the Allies liberated Antwerp and Brussels. *Photo from the National Archives. Identifier: 531213.*

In December 1944, a lanky GI, with hands clasped behind his head, leads a file of American prisoners marching along a road somewhere on the western front. Germans captured these American soldiers during the surprise enemy drive into Allied positions. *Photo from the National Archives. Identifier: 531236.*

The Western Allied invasion of Germany began when the Allies crossed the Rhine River from the West and marched right through the Siegfried Line. The occupation was accomplished by January 17, 1945, when the German Army withdrew from the Ardennes. *Photo from the National Archives. Identifier: 535984.*

For days, the Marines of the 5th Division inched their way up a slope on Red Beach No. 1 toward Surbachi Yama and finally raise the flag over Iwo Jima on February 23, 1945. Photo by Joe Rosenthal, Associated Press. *Photo from National Archives. Identifier: 520748.*

After the fall of Germany in May 1945, General Eisenhower, Commanding General of the Allied Forces in the European Theater, inspects the vast collection of priceless pieces of art confiscated and brought to Berlin by the Nazis during World War II. *Photo from the National Archives. Identifier: 531272.*

On August, 29th, gaunt Allied prisoners of war at Aomori camp near Yokohama, Japan, cheer rescuers from U.S. Navy. Waving flags of the United States, Great Britain States, Great Britain, and Holland. *Photo from the National Archives. Identifier: 520992.*

On September 2, 1945, General Douglas MacArthur signs as Supreme Allied Commander during the formal surrender ceremonies on the *USS Missouri* in Tokyo Bay. *Photo from the National Archives. Identifier: 520694.*

WORLD WAR II

AXIS POWERS

Germany, **Italy**, **Japan**
Hungary, Romania, Bulgaria

versus

ALLIED POWERS

United States, Britain, France, USSR
Australia, Belgium, Brazil, Canada, China, Denmark, Greece,
Netherlands, New Zealand, Norway, Poland, South Africa,
Yugoslavia

APPENDIX E: Strength of Allied and Axis Armed Forces

A summary of the peak strength of the opposing forces during World War II.

Principal Allied Forces: United States, Britain, and France
Principal Axis Forces: German, Japan, and Italy

U.S.S.R.	12,500,000
United States	12,364,000
Germany	10,000,000
Japan	6,095,000
France	5,000,000
Britain	4,683,000
Italy	4,500,000
China (Nationalist)	3,800,000
India	2,150,000
China (Communist)	1,200,000
Poland	1,000,000
Spain	850,000
Turkey	850,000
Belgium	800,000
Canada	780,000
Australia	680,000

1940 World Population:
2,370,000,000

WW II Allied & Axis Forces:
73,272,000 (3% of world population.)

"I feel that it is important for people to know that there was more to Druce than was printed in the paper decades ago. She was extremely intelligent and read a book a day. She was also a loving mother, friendly, and very artistic – she played four different musical instruments and was an avid drawer."

Melinda Nethaway, Shirley Druce's daughter-in-law, in an interview with the Owosso *Argus-Press.*

APPENDIX F: POW Camp Near Owosso Recalled

The Escapee Incident that Drew International Attention by Jim Dingwall, Former Owosso *Argus-Press* City Editor, June 28, 1962. (Reproduced with permission of Tom Campbell, Publisher, *Argus-Press*, Owosso, MI)

The recent death of former Sheriff Charles Downer in Durand recalls an incident that happened during World War II while he was under sheriff. The story was read all over the world, wherever American troops were stationed and wherever the service newspaper, *Stars and Stripes,* was circulated.

It was the escape of two German prisoners of war whose getaway was aided by two women. Freedom for the four was short-lived because in less than 12 hours after they escaped, they were locked in the county jail, thanks to the patient and thorough search made by Downer and Sheriff Ray Gellatly, now an Owosso city commissioner, after the State Police had given up.

Most persons, living here at the time, have probably forgotten that there was a POW camp located at M-21 and the Carland Road, where the car racetrack was located. And newcomers, probably never heard of the camp. But it was a big one, and housed at various times from 300 to 900 Germans, captured on the battlefields of Europe and Africa.

To make use of the labor of the prisoners and keep their thoughts off the fact that they were prisoners, the government started using them as laborers under the Emergency Farm Administration Labor Program.

Eldon Barrett of Owosso was in charge of assigning the groups of prisoners to various farms. With so many American boys in the service, the labor of the prisoners proved a boon in many ways.

They were assigned to various farms to help harvest crops and to the Roach Canning Company plant just off Corunna Avenue. Corn, peas, and tomatoes were canned there, and daily truckloads of prisoners were hauled to the plant to work. As they rode through town, they would sing and holler and wave to everyone they saw.

They apparently enjoyed being prisoners, far from the battlefields overseas. But there was one thing they insisted on having, that was their allotment of beer. "No beer, no work," they would tell farmers who hadn't laid in a supply for them. "Most of them were good workers," Barrett said.

The incident, that drew attention of American service men all over the world and brought down the wrath of servicemen in particular on the heads of Sheriff Gellaty and the late J. Edwin Ellis, who was mayor then, occurred at the canning plant.

The two prisoners managed to slip out of the plant by the back door and make their way to Monroe Street. There the two women were waiting for them in a car, driven by the younger sister of one of them. They were whisked away.

Their absence was not immediately noted. The first Sheriff Gellaty knew of the escape was when his brother-in-law, who was employed at the plant, telephoned him. The State Police were called in, and Gellatly alerted his entire crew of men. The countryside was combed, but to no avail. Around midnight, the State Police gave up the search.

But Downer and Gellatly stuck to their task. They contacted the driver of the car. She told them that when she stopped in Woodhull Township the four got out. She drove away and left them near Colby Lake.

Gellatly and Downer combed the entire area, through brush and swamp. Just before daylight, they sighted the four lying in a thicket. The two officers crept up slowly on the quartet, then suddenly pulled their guns on them. The four submitted meekly to arrest.

This writer was at the county jail when the two officers brought in the four. They were the most bedraggled quartet I have ever seen. The late Art Elliott, circulation manager of the *Argus-Press,* was doubling as photographer for the paper, and we summoned him.

As he was about to snap the pictures of the four with Gellatly and Downer beside them, someone questioned our right to take pictures, inasmuch as the men were POWs. But we told Elliott to snap it, and we would find out later about our right to do so.

Afterwards we called an army officer in Detroit. He asked whose custody the prisoners were in, the army or the sheriff. He okayed it, but said that if the army had been in control, this would have not been permitted.

As for the prisoners, they were returned to the camp here and later transferred to another POW camp. The girls were prosecuted in the federal court and served time in a federal prison.

But the story put on the Associated Press wires, along with the picture, went all over the world in the *Stars and Stripes*. Soon Sherriff Gellatly and Mayor Ellis began getting letters from angry servicemen berating them for letting the prisoners escape. As a matter of fact, they had no more to do with the prison camp than any citizen.

The camp itself was an interesting place. I spent one whole day there, with the army of photographers. The prisoners for the most part were housed in tents, and it was surprising how cozy some of them fixed up their tents. Some even had small gardens. Others planted flowers.

The cooking was done over an underground stove, and some of the food that the cooks turned out made one's mouth water. There was a chapel where men could worship or meditate, and a larger playground where they played ball or other games.

All of them, of course, were captured on the field of battle and most of them were well behaved. But some of them got out-of-line and were immediately transferred to the guard house.

Included among the prisoners were common laborers and professional men, such as doctors, dentists, lawyers, and such. One had operated a beauty parlor in Berlin before the war.

There were some pathetic scenes at the camp, as the fighting in Europe continued. Barrett, who was close to many of the prisoners because of his job, recalls one such incident.

The American forces were shelling a city in Germany and taking a heavy toll of life. One prisoner, a middle-aged German, came to Barrett for information about the battle and sobbed as he told Barrett: "My wife and five children are living in that city. I am praying that their lives are spared."

Strangely enough, the German boys had some attraction for the American girls who used to congregate nights at the wire fence bordering the east side of the camp on Carland Road. Almost nightly, the gals could be seen talking with the prisoners, some of whom would roll out under the fence and visit the girls, then crawl back.

Barrett remembers that the camp had two or three commanders who were inclined to be lenient with the prisoners, or through sheer inability, were unable to keep everybody in line. But this all ended when the army sent in a grizzly veteran of the tortuous battle of Anzio Beach. He straightened this out in a hurry.

As the War wore on, Barrett said that one could notice the difference in the ages of the prisoners, reflecting the drain on the manpower of Germany. Among the first prisoners to arrive here were young men from General Rommel's army in Africa., but before the War was over, men in their 50s were being sent to camp here. One was 68 years old, Barrett remembered.

Prisoners had to volunteer to work before they could be assigned to any job outside the camp. Most of them were glad to get away from camp and enjoy the comparative freedom of working in the fields.

As a result, there was only one strike, staged by one man. He refused to work and was immediately returned to camp. But that night, he was put to work digging a hole six feet square and six feet deep, and then he had to turn around and fill it up. That cured him quickly.

Barrett estimates that between two and three million man-hours of work were put in by the prisoners during the two-and one-half seasons that the camp operated. It was financed by three firms – the Roach Canning Company, the Michigan Sugar Beet Company, and Aunt Jane's Foods.

The program here was among the first to be so operated in the U.S. and was under the general direction of A.B. Love, state emergency farm labor administrator. It was so successful that 18 other states sent representatives to study the operation.

Incidentally, the camp was not maintained in the winter, and the prisoners were transferred to camps in the South. However, some were transferred to Northern Michigan to work in the woods and were housed in heated barracks.

Author's Note. I was surprised when Mr. Dingwall, former City Editor, failed to name the two young women who assisted the POWs to escape. In my research of the Argus-Press *archives, I found seven detailed articles and photos printed between the summer of 1944 and the winter of 1945. These described in great detail the actions of Kitty Case and Shirley Druce, their initial arrest by the Shiawassee County Sheriff, their release from custody the next day, their subsequent re-arrest by the FBI, and their trial, which ended in each being found guilty and sentenced to over a year in prison.*

Oddly enough, an edition of the Argus-Press *dated January 19, 2010 featured a front-page article entitled,* Bound by Her Secret History. *The article describes the life of Shirley Druce after her release from prison. She immediately moved to California, where she married Melvin Nethaway, to whom Druce revealed her past record of the arrest, trial, and subsequent prison term.*

The couple had four children, but the children were never told the story of their mother's past. During her life in California, Druce apparently suffered from alcoholism, causing her relatively early death at the age of forty-seven from cirrhosis of the liver in 1975. After her death, her husband revealed the truth to their children.

A massive brick chimney is the largest remaining structure from the Crossville POW camp in Tennessee. Gerhard Hennes, a German officer, was captured in North Africa in 1943. Five months later, he entered Camp Crossville where he was imprisoned for two years. A WW II bizarre coincidence, Hennes was a prisoner at the same camp as his father, Friedrich Hennes, who was captured by Americans in Europe in the fall of 1944.

After the War, Hennes returned to America and became a citizen. In 2004, he authored *The Barbed Wire: POW in the USA,* in which he presents a detailed description of life at Camp Crossville. *Photo courtesy of* Tennessee History for Kids.

APPENDIX G: POW Camps in Tennessee

- **Camp Crossville, Crossville, TN** (Base Camp)
- **Camp Forrest, Tullahoma, TN** (Base Camp)
- Camp Forrest Hospital, Tullahoma, TN
- Camp Huntsville, Huntsville, TN
- Camp Jackson, Madison County, TN
- Kennedy Army Hospital, Shelby County, TN
- Camp McKeller Field, Madison County, TN
- **Memphis ASF Depot, Shelby County, TN** (Base Camp)
- P.W. General Hospital #2, Camp Forrest, TN
- Pigeon Forge, Sevier County, TN
- Stark General Hospital, Nashville, TN
- Camp Tellico Plains, Monroe County, TN
- Thayer General Hospital, Nashville, TN
- **Camp Tyson, Routon, TN** (Base Camp)

At a POW camp on the outskirts of Owosso, Michigan, German POWs are paid in canteen coupons by Camp Commander Captain Ohrt. At back right are bleachers for the Owosso Speedway race track, which before the War, occupied the area on which Camp Owosso was built. *Photo from the National Archives.*

APPENDIX H. POW Camps in Michigan

- Camp Allegan
- Camp Au Train
- Camp Barryton, Mecosta County
- Camp Benton Harbor, Berrien Count
- Camp Blissfield, Lenawee County
- Camp Caro, Tuscola County
- Camp Columa, Berrien County
- Camp Crosswell, Sanilac County
- **Fort Custer, Galesburg** (Base Camp)
- Camp Dundee, Monroe County
- Camp Evelyn, Alger County
- Camp Freeland, Saginaw County
- Camp Fremont, Newaygo County
- Camp Germfask
- Camp Grant, Newaygo County
- Camp Grosse Ile Township, Wayne County
- Camp Hart, Oceana County
- Camp Lake Odessa, Ionia County
- Camp Mattawan, Van Buren County
- Camp Mass, Ontonagon County
- Camp Milan (USFR), Monroe & Washtenaw Counties
- Camp Odessa Lakes, Tuscola County
- Camp Owosso, Shiawassee County
- Camp Pori, Upper Peninsula
- Camp Raco, Upper Peninsula near Sault Ste. Marie
- Camp Romulus Army Airfield, Wayne County
- Camp Shelby, Oceana County
- Camp Sidnaw
- Camp Wayne (Fort), Detroit, Wayne County

Made in the USA
Columbia, SC
30 October 2021